STR...
Happenings

1·99

STRANGE HAPPENINGS

by

Paul Bannister

Publishers · GROSSET & DUNLAP · New York
A FILMWAYS COMPANY

For Jennie, Claire, and Rachel: my three blondes.

To those good friends whose help, counsel, and sound common sense made this book possible: my deepest thanks.

To my friends and colleagues at the National ENQUIRER, my thanks and gratitude for years of assistance. Special thanks to Iain Calder, for permission to use ENQUIRER photographs; to Bonnie Jones for photo research; to Paul Levy for sound, sane advice; and to Ron Caylor for tending my neuroses through four years of assignments.

Copyright © 1978 by Paul Bannister
All rights reserved
Published simultaneously in Canada
Library of Congress catalog card number: 77-87112
ISBN 0-448-14390-9 (hardcover)
ISBN 0-448-14391-7 (paperback)
First printing
Printed in the United States of America

CONTENTS

INTRODUCTION

A shadowy, half-seen shape caught the woman's attention as she sat sewing in her living room. She turned with a familiar shudder of horror. Nothing was there. But as she watched, her eyes widening in terror, the fabric of the couch ripped apart as if raked by giant, razor-sharp claws.

She knew it was the same creature that had been plaguing her family for three long years. An ape-like entity from another world, it was a familiar—a demoniac animal-thing sent by a black magician.

This was the creature that had systematically opened cuts on her face every time she slept, thin razor-like cuts that came three or four at a time, sometimes even opening before the horrified eyes of her helpless family.

This was the creature that had ripped a healthy tooth from her mouth as she slept, destroyed her home with spontaneous fires, and ripped apart her furniture coverings, mattresses, clothes, shoes. Even the family Bible was slashed in cross-shaped ribbons.

Such events are still happening today all over the world. Scientists who have investigated them are baffled. All they can say is, "Black magic must be real. We believe black magicians can put spells on people and use unknown forces to cause such phenomena."

This particular case began in Guarulhos, a suburb of São Paulo, Brazil, in 1973. It is still going on, although the family has moved their home twice and now live in Greater São Paulo—a city of 11 million people. I am a journalist with an interest in the paranormal, and when I read scientific papers presented at an international conference in Tokyo in 1977, I decided to visit the Brazilian group who reported on the Guarulhos poltergeist.

Hernani Andrade, sixty-four, is president of the Brazilian Institute for Psychobiophysical Research, has been professor of physics at the University of São Paulo for twenty-eight years, and has some sixty-one similar poltergeist cases in his files. "This one is a good one because the family has not employed a black magician to remove the evil action, so it has continued for a long time," he explained.

"In the great majority of cases we have investigated, the troubles have been brought on after quarrels, love matters, business problems, disputes, and the like. Frequently the victim does not know when or how he unleashed revenge from those who are attacking him—but the consequences are usually terrible."

The Guarulhos victims, Maria and Manuel X, are religious people. They belong to an evangelistic sect, and because of their commitment they are reluctant to use black magicians. The scientists found this reluctance a vital key, because it enabled them to make first-hand observations for several years. The research director of the Institute, Carmen Marinho, told me, "We have seen upholstery opening, but there has been nobody and nothing nearby to do it. I myself have seen animal shapes, like a monkey. They were not real animals but elementals, entities sent by sorcerers. Some have reddish fur, short and shiny; others have greyish fur. They are real, not imagined."

In other incidents, the São Paulo group has documented all kinds of odd events: homes bombarded with stones that appeared from nowhere (some even came from within closed rooms), lighted candles, used in black magic rituals for the dead, materializing from thin air; fires that break out mysteriously, even on bare plaster walls. In one startling case, a young girl's clothes burned to ashes in a drawer while her sister's, folded up with them, were unharmed—and didn't even smell of smoke.

Usually the uncanny attacks ended after a black magician was hired to take the spell off the family. "These cases are evidence of the astounding mental powers in our world," Professor Andrade warns. And I believe he is right.

Astonishing events happen every day. Some we can explain, some we cannot. At the same conference in Japan at which the Brazilian scientists outlined their findings, a French psychic—Jean Pierre Giraud—demonstrated some of the extraordinary mental powers certain people possess.

Without touching it, he made a two-ounce plastic cylinder skid across a tabletop. Then, under cheat-proof conditions laid down by the 75 researchers who were watching, he also made a compass needle turn at his command. Giraud has been rigorously tested for seven years. To him, feats of unbelieveable mind-power are routine.

All of us have insights into the power of the super-minds. We sometimes have those intuitive glimpses when we just *know* what's going to happen next. Will we find, in the next few decades, that we will be able to project our minds far out of our bodies, across the expanse of limitless space? Will we find that perhaps we are not alone, even on this planet? Will we find that ghosts are real, that perhaps they are time travelers from our past, or will we find they are lingering echoes of the agony of some forgotten horror?

Of course, scientists around the world are anxious to see whether there are new energy potentials in psychic research. The American government's own Central Intelligence Agency is closely watching developments like telepathy from a submarine. Experiments carried out in the summer of 1977 seem to defy the principles of physics.

A secret report of Soviet activity reveals that they are training Tibetan monks to kill or induce madness simply by mind-power. This exactly parallels United States research in microwaves that has not yet reached the columns of our daily newspapers. So perhaps truth really is stranger than fiction.

Consider this: a troop of Roman soldiers, dead for close to 1600 years, is still marching its lonely way along a roadway long since buried. Witnesses have seen the men and described in accurate detail facts that historians did not know until later. Why is this doomed platoon of men, dispiritedly shuffling along, still visible to modern eyes?

Consider this: a chair in an English hostelry still carries a deadly curse. Everyone who sits in it dies, usually within forty-eight hours, sometimes sooner. Is this a relic of black magic, invoked by someone with powerful evil intent? The chair of death has claimed victims who scoffed. Why? And how?

Consider this: UFO crews seem to be using increased brutality and callousness towards their human captives. Time and again, people who report UFO contact claim to have undergone painful, humiliating 'medical examinations' by mysterious aliens. Whereas these meetings once were described as gentle experiences, recent contacts seem to be terrifying events, nightmare horrors. Are we in danger of becoming a subject race to some technically advanced alien civilization?

Ours is a small, wonderful planet, but mysterious things are happening on it.

CHAPTER. 1.

WHAT'S ALL THIS ABOUT GHOSTS?

Busby's Chair

Local people call it the "Chair of Death," and its owner is so fearful of the chair that he has locked it away in an old coach house.

For the hard-headed, unsuperstitious folk of the North Riding of Yorkshire, England, believe that a hanged man's chair carries a 275-year-old curse. Sudden death awaits anyone who would sit in that chair. To date, say the locals, the chair has killed seven people.

The owner faces an agonizing decision: should he keep the chair intact, risking more deaths, or should he destroy it and risk death himself?

The story begins in 1702 in a coaching inn at the side of the dusty Great North Road from London to Edinburgh. A burly Yorkshireman, whose name has come down to us only as Busby, was a regular at the inn. He lived with his father-in-law, Dan Oty, half a mile away, at a farmhouse grandly called Danoty Hall.

Both men were coiners, clipping and skimming silver from coins in order to make forgeries of their own. Busby was a man of violent temper. Other regulars at the inn, then called Sand Hutton Inn, after the tiny hamlet around it, knew all about Busby's temper. They also knew that the straight-backed oak armchair in the inn was for him alone.

One night, Busby left the inn drunk and truculent. He went home and fought Dan Oty, killing him with a spade. Arrested almost at once, he was sentenced to be hanged in chains. The gibbet stood at the same crossroads as the inn.

It was the custom of the times for a condemned man to be allowed a last drink—in fact the drink was often drugged to ease the man's dying. Busby sat in his oak chair and drank from his own tankard before

walking the few steps to the waiting scaffold. After his death, his body was left to rot in its chains as a warning to other evildoers. Custom also decreed that, after a suitable time of exposure, the remains of a hanged man be buried in the shadow of the gibbet, or *stoop*, which is the local dialect word for scaffold.

Busby's execution is still remembered in the history of the locals. For they say that the curse was put on Busby's chair when he left it for the last time.

"He promised sudden death to anyone who dared use it," says the inn's present landlord, Anthony Earnshaw. "I am convinced that chair has something evil about it. There have been just too many coincidences and scary experiences. I believe in the curse. I want nothing to do with that chair."

Earnshaw showed me the chair, a large, square armchair, its oak blackened by centuries. He had it secured away in a back coach house, under several heavy wooden crates. "Nobody is going to sit in that chair again," he says.

As he made this statement, the landlord turned pale. For in the six years Earnshaw has owned the tavern, now known as the Busby Stoop, seven people have died in that chair, and the last two were personal friends of the genial innkeeper.

The first deaths known personally by Earnshaw were of two young airmen. They had heard the old story, scoffed at it, and had come to the inn to sit in the chair, which was then kept roped off in a corner of the bar. Having sat in Busby's chair, the young men left the inn a bit later. Both died in a car wreck three miles south of the inn when their sports car smashed into a tree.

"Soon after I became licensee," recalls Earnshaw, "there was a big, athletic army sergeant-major in here, drinking with some other soldiers. They had all read the story—it's in a frame there on the wall—and the sergeant-major insisted on bringing the chair out of its corner and sitting in it for the evening.

"Two weeks later one of the soldiers came in. The sergeant-major, a big, healthy chap who never had a day's illness in his life, had dropped dead three days after he was here."

Anthony Earnshaw, tavernkeeper of the Busby Stoop, Yorkshire, England, looks at the "Chair of Death" and is as baffled as everyone else in the area. The chair, which is now kept under lock and key in a coach house at the rear of the ancient inn, is reputed to have caused scores of deaths in its 300-year history.

Earnshaw wiped at the bar top, then went on with his story. "Last year, they were building some new houses about a mile away. Some bricklayers came in at lunchtime. One of them, a young lad of seventeen, took up a dare to sit in the chair. Two hours later, he fell from some scaffolding and was killed. His father came in after the funeral and pleaded with me to destroy the chair. I was afraid to do it. But I was so shaken, I put the chair in the cellar.

"Four months ago, a very good friend of mine came in with another man. They asked to see the chair. I took them down to the cellar, but one of the girls called down to me a moment later. I was wanted on the telephone in the bar. When I went back into the cellar, my friend was whitefaced and shaken.

"He said the other man had sat in the chair and, as he did so, he had felt a sense of evil. That was a Friday night. The following Tuesday morning, the man who sat in the chair dropped dead in Ripon marketplace. He was forty-two years old and in good health. That was when I put Busby's chair under lock and key.

"Even that wasn't enough. Another friend, Harry, a fellow member of my Masonic lodge, heard about the chair and wanted to see it. He persuaded me to show it to him, but only after he promised not to sit in it.

"Well, I showed it to him, and we were about to leave the coach house when I was called to the kitchen. One of the barmaids had cut her hand. I rushed off, not thinking. When I came back, Harry was laughing. He told me he had broken his promise and sat in the chair. He was found dead less than forty-eight hours later."

I looked up the local death records for these six cases and substantiated them. I then checked on the seventh case, that of a woman who worked at the tavern and who had stumbled back into the chair while she was cleaning. She died within a month of a brain tumor.

The vicar of Thirsk, a no-nonsense, former army padre, is the Reverend Joseph Mainwaring-Taylor. I met him outside his medieval church of St. Mary the Virgin, in bright sunshine. We talked about the chair, and he solemnly said: "Certainly I believe the chair has evil about it. It should be soaked in petrol and burned. I have tried to exorcise it, but without result.

"There are many strange and unexplained things in this world, some of them evil. I believe this chair is one of them. It could well contain some echo of Busby's malevolence, some remainder of his personality."

Can this be so? Can some survival of our personality hold on to a link between times past and present? No one has ever claimed to have seen Busby's ghost, although heavy footsteps haunt the inn, say the regulars, after the bar is officially closed.

But can such things be true? I don't know. Busby's is one of the best-documented cases I have ever looked into, and I confess that the sight of that chair made the hair prickle on the back of my neck....

The Roman Legion

Not far from the Busby Stoop, forty miles down the road in York, I came across one of the most dramatic ghost stories I have ever heard, from one of the best witnesses I have ever met.

Police constable Harry Martindale is a man of whom the British police force can feel proud. A big man, six feet four inches and 250 pounds, Martindale has hands like shovels and a careful, even ponderous manner. He prides himself on being unimaginative, for he is solid and unshakable. Yet, in the damp, earth-floored cellar of a medieval building, the Treasurer's House in York, Martindale crouched in terror as he watched the apparition of a troop of Roman soldiers trudge past him and on through the wall.

Harry Martindale was not at that time a policeman. He was working as a heating engineer and was on a job in the old cellar, repairing some overhead pipes. "I heard a sort of tinny trumpet call," he told me, as we crouched in the ancient cellar with local historian John Mitchell.

"I looked around, and a smallish soldier wearing a kilt and carrying a sort of trumpet came out of that wall over there. He ignored me and shuffled diagonally across the cellar toward the opposite wall. But before he disappeared, another soldier, on a ragged-looking pony, followed him. Behind them came about fourteen or sixteen more men, in double file. I fell from my stepladder and cowered against the corner, but they ignored me.

"The oddest thing was that they were all marching thigh-deep in the floor. Only in one spot, where someone had dug away part of the floor, could I see their feet."

Harry described the phantom soldiers in detail. They had round shields and wore hand-dyed woolen kilts of streaky green. They had an assortment of equipment, from short stabbing swords to throwing spears. Most had leather helmets. The officer on horseback had a few plumes in his crested helmet. The sandals they were wearing had knee-high thongs. The trumpeter's instrument was long and curving and seemed to be made of brass.

Harry's overall impression of the soldiers was that they were "seedy." "They sort of shuffled along, dispiritedly. I reckoned they were Roman soldiers[York is the site of an ancient Roman camp, then called Eboracium], but they didn't look like Charlton Heston in polished, shining armor."

Police Constable Harry Martindale
kneels in the cellar under the old
Treasurer's House, York, where once he
saw the ghosts of Roman legionnaires
march past.

Constable Martindale shows the author the very solid walls through which the remnant of the Roman troop disappeared.

Even after the last soldier had disappeared through the wall, Harry remained crouched in his safe corner for several minutes before dashing out of the cellar and up to daylight. He told nobody about the apparition for a couple of days, but by a happy chance he then confided in a local historian. The historian took careful note of everything Harry had to say, pointing out that the hole in the cellar floor was made by archeologists who were excavating a section of the old Roman road. But the historian also assured Harry that he had imagined the whole thing because he had described the shield shapes wrong. Roman infantry never had round shields.

And there the matter lay.

Dramatically, exactly seven years after that sighting, two archeologists—whose names, irritatingly, are not on public record—were in the same cellar, examining the foundations of Treasurer's House, when the same apparition marched through, again with a trumpet blast.

Someone remembered Harry's account, looked it up, and compared it with the archeologists' story. It matched in every detail. Meanwhile, in the intervening seven years, an apparently unimportant piece of information about the composition of the VIth Legion had come to light. The legion, which was withdrawn from York in the fourth century as the Roman Empire crumbled, had been bolstered by auxiliaries with round shields.

Says Constable Martindale in his quiet manner: "I believe I saw a troop of those auxiliaries, marching out on some hopeless foray in which they were all to die. The reason I saw them thigh-deep in the floor was because their spirits were still marching on the surface of the now-buried Roman road."

Could this be some leftover relic of psychic agony? Did the despairing thoughts of those about-to-die auxiliaries somehow become trapped in time and space, to be seen by three modern men? I don't know. But there is a parallel case, another story that I investigated in England. It was less dramatic, yet it was still a compelling account that could lend support to those who believe in the survival of consciousness.

Nell Gwynne

Walter Goldsmith is an English gentleman. A former Royal Air Force fighter pilot, he is the present owner of a fifteenth-century manor house built on the site of a ruined Norman castle.

From the fine, mullioned windows at the front of his house, look across the moat, across the lawn, and out to the spires of St. Albans. Look to your right, and just by the moat is an old stone building. Legend says that King Charles II kept his beautiful, laughing lover, Nell Gwynne, in that cottage. The manor house, Salisbury Hall, long a Royalist house, is said to have been one of Charles's favorite country retreats.

Walter Goldsmith, who has put together a fine RAF museum in an ancient barn at the rear of the old house, believes that the laughing ghost of beautiful Nell, the one-time orange seller who captured a king's heart, still haunts his home. He tells of seeing a young girl sweeping around a corner; of people who once lived in the hall meeting her on the stairs—a lovely, smiling girl. A number of people, including himself, have heard her laughter echo happily through the house. He says the very atmosphere sometimes seems to lift and lighten when even her name is mentioned.

Walter adds: "Our favorite story is that Nell gave birth in that cottage by the moat to the king's son. He was riding by, and in jest she held the infant out of the upper window in her arms and threatened to throw him into the moat.

"The king is supposed to have called out, 'By God, Nellie, take care of my young Duke of St. Albans'—bestowing a title on his bastard as fast as his eye could light on the church spire over there, for inspiration.

"I do know that we have heard her laughter, in daylight as well as at night, and it is a lovely, pleasing sound."

The same hall has another, tragic ghost. Goldsmith says: "We have all in this family heard the sound of a man's dragging footsteps going along a corridor upstairs and through a wall where there used to be a door. The legends say that a wounded Royalist escaped from the Government soldiers at the battle of St. Albans, and that he took refuge here. But he was so despairing and so unwilling to be captured that he shot himself with his own horse pistol. Now, when alterations were made to that part of the house, we found an old door with a heavy lock. It was jammed—jammed by the ball of a horse pistol...."

The Pesky Ones

Alf Taylor is eighty years old and one of the most reluctant people I have ever interviewed. I found him through some solid detective work after I had heard of his strange part at a parapsychology convention in Holland and resolved to meet him.

For months, Alf and his gardening supplies hut were the center of a poltergeist's attack. *Poltergeist* is a German word for "noisy ghost" and is one of the more disturbing psychic phenomena. Typically, when a poltergeist is about, objects are moved or hurled about; sometimes strange noises and smells occur. It's very upsetting for the victim. Various researchers believe that the poltergeist is a force induced by the "agent," in this case Alf himself. But nobody knows for sure.

In the entrance hall of their stately home, Salisbury Hall, near St. Albans, England, stand Mr. and Mrs. Oliver Goldsmith. Fortunately, they are not in the least distressed that Nell Gwynne, a king's mistress, has been seen on the stairway behind them.

Photograph courtesy of the National ENQUIRER.

Alf's case was particularly interesting because a first-rate English psychic researcher personally witnessed some of the events, as did about thirty other people during the six months they continued. Alf is treasurer of the Downham Garden and Allotments Guild, a gardening association in Bromley, Kent, whose members grow produce for profit. Here is his story as he related it to me.

"Soon after workmen began to lay the foundations for garages next door to our gardening store, odd things started happening. Handfuls of granulated fertilizer, materializing from nowhere, would fall on me or on other people.

"A tin mug we used for measuring kept mysteriously filling up with the fertilizer even though nobody was near it. Time after time, objects would hurl themselves across the store—seeming to come from blank walls. Weights of two, seven, even fourteen pounds frequently flew across the room, although they had no force when they hit you.

"I found things buried in the fertilizer bins, although there was no chance for anyone to have tampered with them. Once, a deliveryman brought twenty sacks of fertilizer and left them on the ground outside the hut. They were fine as I walked past to go into the store. But when I walked straight out again, no more than five seconds later, every one of them was slashed open, in the shape of a perfect cross. Yet nobody had the time to do it and escape unseen.

"I have watched taps twist themselves on after I'd turned them off. Once that same liquid fertilizer made a devil's face on the door, and although it was liquid, it didn't flow down the door until I shouted for help. Another time, a deliveryman came with some fifty-pound sacks, two dozen of them, and while he was talking in the store, they unloaded themselves. There wasn't time for anyone to do it, and there wasn't a sound, although we were only a few feet away from the truck and should have heard...."

Alf's wife, Mona, told me how she had water shower down on her while she was sitting in her living room; how golf balls had plopped down gently next to her lawn chair when she was resting, although nobody was near; and how coins had tumbled around her when she was in a locked room.

But the most convincing testimony came from independent wit-

John Hammond (left) and Alf Taylor, outside a London gardening store. In his left hand Hammond displays a weight that flew across the store by itself. In his right hand, understandably, he is holding a padlock.

nesses. Manfred Cassirer, chairman of the Physical Phenomena Committee of the respected London-based Society for Psychical Research, declared: "This was an extremely interesting case of apparently genuine paranormal phenomena. It was a very complex case and I personally observed some amazing phenomena."

He had seen showers of fertilizer fall in inaccessible places in the garden store; he had observed money that Alf had counted scatter, sometimes upward; he had watched a plastic beaker fly out from a blank wall and hit his wife on the head; and had stared in wonder as a chalked cross appeared on the floor without anyone being near.

"One very startling thing happened during my investigation," he recalled. "It was the formation of a face in chemicals on the counter of the store. The face was three-dimensional and would have taken some considerable time to form normally—but it happened very quickly. I am certain it was a paranormal event."

I spoke with other witnesses who had been pushed in the back by some mysterious force or had seen lumps of clay whiz past their ears. One Irish worker was hit on the head by a brick that "just floated" slowly toward him.

Today, the disturbances in Kent are over, for the time being at least. But they are being duplicated in other parts of the world....

In Detroit, university researchers were baffled by these antics by a poltergeist: a bellows-type door "exploded" open as a professor walked by; a chair tilted backward, gathering speed as it went, and then slammed into a wall; and a white-gloved hand knocked at doors and windows.

Joseph G. Pratt, a professor at the University of Virginia, is a cautious researcher who personally witnessed a variety of poltergeist activities that were even stranger. Here is his story:

"A grandmother and granddaughter were together in the kitchen. Either simultaneously or in rapid succession, a 'pull-out' type of stove moved back and forth from the wall; the dishwasher and refrigerator doors opened and closed; the drawers under the sink opened; the chairs moved out from the kitchen table; and a stool from the other side of the room slid across the floor, pinning the two women into a corner."

When they went back into the house later, the grandmother felt a very hard slap on her behind and heard a voice telling her: "Go away. Go far away."

The family sought religious help, but during an exorcism a candle flew over the children's heads and chests of drawers tipped over. Eventually the poltergeist activity stopped. Researchers speculated that one or both of the children in the house had caused the disturbances by some paranormal means, but no conclusions were reached.

I met the same problem in a small mining town in Pennsylvania. I went to Minersville to meet the parish priest of the Eastern Orthodox Church there, after I heard of an exorcism he had attempted.

The story started when the son of a local businessman became interested in black magic, and one night, as he put it, "brought the devil home with me." After that the house was filled with supernatural sounds, often deep-throated growling or wild laughter. The teen-aged son and daughter both experienced unsettling events. The daughter recalls them in this manner:

"I would be woken up, usually about three A.M., by tappings on my shoulder or knee. Then, one time, I felt a pressure starting to push me against the cushions. I couldn't scream. I couldn't move. My head was bursting with pain. I could hear people talking all around me, but I couldn't distinguish what they were saying. I lay pinned like that for more than an hour, until my brother came in."

The girl also reported that she saw a dark-skinned, bearded man standing over her one night; another time, she woke to find a gray-haired, homely-looking woman beckoning to her to follow.

The girl's mother, a senior nurse at a large hospital, was pushed down the cellar steps by ghostly hands and subjected to mysterious buzzings in her mind and by the appearance of a spinning circle that sapped her strength. The father of the family woke, choking, one night to find the dark-haired, bearded man, apparently the same man his daughter had seen, "attempting to take over my mind and body." The torment of the family's teen-aged son came in the form of uncanny laughter, voices and shadows, which plagued him for more than a month.

Eventually the local priest, the Right Reverend Archimandrite Robert Demetrio, performed an exorcism. "A sigh seemed to pass through the house," recalled his cantor, John Walker, "and the atmosphere changed." The strange happenings ended forthwith.

Philip Who Never Was

Montreal was cold. The Canadiens, Montreal's ice-hockey team, were losing, about to end a 21-game winning streak. In the streets, snow-banks of dirt-encrusted frozen matter were more ice than snow. And in the cozy bar of the once-elegant Mount Royal hotel, I sat with a compelling yet relaxed man, George Owen, a professor at the University of Toronto. Professor Owen was discussing a movie he had just shown to an audience of 1,200 people.

"We created a ghost," he explained simply. "We chose to do it, and we did. It was an interesting, entertaining, and academically satisfying thing to do."

They had called the ghost Philip. With one *L*. He was a completely fictitious person. He never existed and never could have existed in the extremely specific set of circumstances with which the Toronto group had invested in him.

But Philip was real all right. He was real enough to move tables, to answer questions in a truly Victorian parlor-game sort of way, and to manifest a force completely unexplained by modern science. Philip was a game, a mind game so exciting, so uncanny, and so real that psychic researchers around the world have been forced to take notice of the Philip who never was.

As George Owen outlined the fantastic story of the group who made a ghost, he undermined every apparition story I'd ever heard—yet there was no apparition. He supported every psychokinetic story I'd ever heard—and I was entranced. For Philip was and is an excellent example of mindpower.

One of my regrets is that I never met Philip. But I met his maker, which is, I suppose, more than most of us can say. I'll qualify that one more time: I met *one* of his makers. Because Philip was made by a group of people, and they made him as a joke.

Eight men and women, none of them spiritualists, all of them "average" in that their occupations cross the spectrum of society, chose to make a ghost. To date—and they are still trying even as you read this page—they have not managed to make Philip appear as an apparition. I believe they will, eventually.

Iris Owen, George's wife, has written a book entitled *Conjuring Up Philip*, which tells the full story. The bare bones are this: The group set out to demonstrate that they could manufacture something, an *unnamed something*, from their group will. And they proceeded to do just that.

They chose a name, a personality, a life story, a time and place in history. To make their experiment more valid, they chose a place that someone had read up about, a time that they had carefully researched, and a person that they knew could *not* have existed. The group knew Philip could not have existed because they placed him in a stately English home during a time which left records of a particular family, but no documentation of such an individual. (To preserve the privacy of the English manor, the Toronto researchers have not revealed its name.) Then, knowing that there could be no such person, they set about communicating with him.

And, against every rule, the personality that they had created came to life.

I do not mean to bore you by stressing exactly how Philip was created. Yet I believe that somewhere in this story is a key to understanding much about the psychic phenomenon of ghosts. For, if Philip was *not* a discarnate being with whom the group was able to communicate, if he was in fact no more than a product of their lively imaginations, then what force was at work? What strange happening took place in Toronto?

The Owens and their friends met at regular intervals. They agreed on Philip's personality and gave their ghost a colorful past, with some overtones of tragedy. They communicated with him by asking him to rap upon the table—and he obligingly did so. The group never sat in darkness, they used cheerful chants and songs, they treated the whole thing as a kind of private joke. But, wait—*joke* is the wrong word. They simply set about *enjoying* what they did.

Obligingly, Philip did the same. He answered with his table rappings, in a very definite manner to the group's strongly felt questions, but only with scratchings on the table when the questions were indecisive. He cheerfully went along with historical inaccuracies (how could he know any better?—he was the product of his makers). Still, even with the inaccuracies, his answers were remarkably consistent. He admitted on one occasion that he had a brewmaster who fell into the vat.

Two members of the group were able to elicit answers from Philip without touching the table; the others had to come into contact with the table. Also, the raps Philip produced on the table (or on a metal sheet sometimes used for the purpose) were different, when analyzed acoustically, from raps produced by human hands. The most dramatic phenomena included Philip making the heavy wooden table used in the experiment follow people around. It attempted to follow George Owen out of the room on one occasion, but was frustrated by the width of the doorway.

As I left the matter with George Owen, the group was attempting to produce an image or hallucination of Philip. I have little doubt that they will succeed. After all, if the group can make a table levitate, make it act apparently independently of the group, make it produce "answers" to their questions, then why shouldn't they be able to produce an image of this ghost they have created?

Is this, in fact, the way we see ghosts?

Postscript on the attempts to create a ghost: At this writing, the Toronto group is still unsuccessful. They are valiantly continuing their experiment. Meanwhile, in Montreal, another group is also trying to create an apparition. They expect their experiment to take several years.

CHAPTER. 2.

some mouinc experiences

**Now You See
It, Now You Don't**

John Hasted, professor of experimental physics and head of the department of physics at Birbeck College, London, is a distinguished scientist of impeccable background. I lunched with him one day in a hotel in Utrecht, Holland. Outside, the small town bustled with market-day crowds. A few barges slid quietly by along the canal, under hump-backed bridges. We sipped Moselle wine and admired the sunshine. And then, quite calmly, Hasted said, "I have personally witnessed dematerialization a number of times, even under test conditions in my laboratory."

Twenty years ago, such a statement would have caused the good professor to be regarded as a crank, someone unfit for a university post. Today, his work is regarded as being at the cutting edge of physics. Typically, he wan't afraid to test controversial Israeli psychic Uri Geller. Geller is the sort of subject many investigators avoid, because of his showmanship.

Again typically, Hasted aimed for the top: he wanted to try to obtain evidence for dematerialization—for making objects disappear. As he related it: "I was supplied by a Cambridge laboratory with a crystal of vanadium carbide, a rather rare and very hard material. I really wanted to see if its structure could be changed by Geller's action."

Before witnesses, Hasted had the specimen put inside a cellulose capsule and laid it on a piece of metal. Geller never went nearer to the capsule than eight inches. The professor put his own hand between Geller's and the target material.

Professor John Hasted, of London, with the key that teleported and the clock that defied the laws of psychics to chime—after Uri Geller visited his home.

"I felt a tingling sensation in my hand," Hasted reported. "I was watching the capsule, and as Geller moved his hand, above mine, suddenly the capsule gave a little jump, like a jumping bean, then another jump. This was seen by everybody.

"Geller stopped concentrating and we looked at the capsule. Only half the crystal was there. We didn't open it then, but sent it back to Cambridge. They identified it as the same crystal. Nothing was changed—except that half of it was now missing."

In another set of baffling incidents, Geller visited the Hasted home briefly—and left a legacy of mysterious happenings.

"For several months, odd things happened," the professor recalled. "A small ivory ornament appeared out of thin air, not flying, but dropping to the ground from about a foot above the floor. There was also the key of a French Empire clock that teleported from one room to the next. I found it on the floor, by the kitchen door, and put it back in its proper place in a glass cabinet in the next room. I walked back into the kitchen and found it lying back in the same place on the floor."

Hasted quickly realized that this was a fine opportunity for some investigation. He kept the key lying in its spot on the floor for nearly three months, first covering it carefully with a pie-dish cover to avoid interfering with its exact placement. His care paid off. By trial and error he found that if his wife, Jocelyn, were to approach the clock, which was in the next room, it would chime—but only if someone was within a few feet of the key on the kitchen floor.

An even more uncanny thing about the clock's chiming was that it defied all known physical laws to do it. For the clock had been prepared for storage, and its mechanisms were bound up with thread. Without breaking that thread, the clock simply could not chime. Yet chime it did, and the thread remained unbroken.

Hasted recalled another remarkable event that happened after Geller's visit. "We had bought a turkey as a Christmas gift for a lawyer friend of ours and had put it on a white-topped kitchen table. Our friend came into the kitchen to look at the turkey, which was dressed and cleaned. There was a plastic bag of giblets next to it. As we looked, the table was clean and clear. The bag of giblets was sealed at the top with wire.

"Suddenly, we all noticed a brown thing on the kitchen table, about two feet from the plastic bag. It was the turkey's liver, and it should have been inside the plastic bag. There was no smear of blood. The liver had just appeared there. The bag was still firmly sealed. We recognized it as an example of dematerialization and rematerialization.

"We checked, of course, to be sure that there wasn't another turkey liver inside the bag. There wasn't. We even took the liver back to the butcher to make sure it *was* a turkey liver and not something else. As far as possible, we made sure it was the same turkey liver."

Geller isn't the only psychic tested by John Hasted who has demonstrated this uncanny ability to defy known laws of physics. In Ontario, Canada, an eighteen-year-old youth, Nicholas X, demonstrated the same ability.

In a stringently controlled test, Nicholas three times moved crystals, which were chosen because of their extreme hardness and for their ability to be "fingerprinted" on an electron microscope, to avoid the possibility of their being exchanged. Nicholas moved the crystals out of double containers, sealed with epoxy resin. Once he actually succeeded in moving a crystal back into its container again.

"These dematerializations happened before my own eyes —although when you watch it you usually miss it, because it is such a tiny movement," Hasted admitted.

"Amazingly, in the case of the crystal that he moved back into the capsule, it was the same one he had moved out. It was there, then it wasn't. We examined it, and the sealed capsule was empty. Then he concentrated, and there it was, back again. We have no idea where it went."

The Case for Sai Baba

John Hasted is not the only European academic with firsthand knowledge of these moving phenomena. He shares this distinction with Hans Bender, director of the Institute for Border Areas of Psi, an adjunct of Freiburg University in West Germany.

Bender's institute is a long, low building set among trees on the side of a steep-rising road. It overlooks the medieval cathedral of the Black Forest township of Freiburg. Bender himself is a tall man, slightly stooped, with an aquiline nose, a mane of white hair, and the long slender hands of a pianist. As he sat in his leather armchair in the gathering dusk of a summer evening, he related this story:

"Although I have never witnessed dematerialization in the laboratory, I have seen a pattern of striking similarities that leaves me personally convinced that concrete, physical objects can penetrate through solid walls into closed rooms.

"Stones, for instance, come into a closed room from outside a house during poltergeist attacks. Witnesses describe the stones falling

> Dr. Hans Bender, the eminent German parapsychologist and researcher from the University of Freiburg.

from about five or six inches below the ceiling. They don't bounce, and when you touch them they are usually warm.

"In one case, here in Bavaria in 1969, stones came into a closed kitchen and objects flew out of the locked house. Some little dolls came out of a closed cupboard, seemingly through the very fabric of the door, and the people saw small bottles—perfume and medicine bottles—coming from the roof of the house. Interestingly, when the bottles were seen coming from the house, they were not falling in a straight line, but in a zigzag fashion, as if they were being transported, not as if they were falling free."

Other researchers have shown keen interest in these mysterious psychokinetic powers. An American, Karlis Osis, research fellow at the New York-based American Society for Psychical Research, and a University of Iceland professor, Erlendur Haraldsson, joined forces for a visit to India, to speak with the religious leader Sri Sathya Sai Baba there. They came away frankly baffled, for during their interviews with Sai Baba, they witnessed fourteen appearances and disappearances of objects. The mystic refused to use his powers for formal experiments, however.

Dr. Osis, Estonian-born, is a careful researcher with decades of experience. Professor Haraldsson, a native Icelander, is head of the department of psychology at his university. Neither man is gullible. Yet they could not explain how Sai Baba could perform the feats that he did.

"We were talking about spiritual values," Osis recalled, and Sai Baba said that the spiritual life should be grown together with daily life, like a double *rudraksha*. We didn't understand the term, and our interpreter could not translate it. Sai Baba made several attempts to explain; then, with a gesture of impatience, he closed his fist and waved his hand. He opened his palm and showed us a double *rudraksha*, which is a rare specimen in nature, like a twin apple or twin orange.

"We admired the specimen and handed it back. He took it, then said he wanted to give Erlendur a present. He enclosed the *rudraksha* in his hands, blew on it, and opened his hands to Erlendur. There was the *rudraksha*, but with a golden ornamented shield on each side of it and a golden cross with a ruby fastened to it."

There was another baffling incident during their meeting with Sai Baba. The mystic became irritable when the two researchers continued to try to persuade him to take part in some formal experiments. He turned to Dr. Osis and said in a commanding tone: "Look at your ring."

The stone from the ring was missing, yet it had been there seconds before. Dr. Osis relates that the stone had been held in place by four small tabs, which protruded over the stone from the oval frame, and by the edges of gold above and below the stone. The tabs that had held the stone were unbent; the frame was unbent. Dr. Osis had been no closer to Sai Baba than a distance of several feet.

"This was *my* experiment," remarked the mystic.

"We considered the phenomena—not just the two incidents we have recounted, but others we saw, such as a flow of holy ash from the down-turned palm of his open hand—probably paranormal," says Dr. Osis cautiously. He and Haraldsson even examined the mystic's robe while he was asleep. But they found no trace of hidden pockets, stage magic, or the like.

The two scientists also talked with witnesses who testified to Sai Baba's ability to produce hot food while traveling by car, to produce fresh fruit that is out of season, and to travel by psychic means and appear in different parts of the continent minutes apart. On one occasion, the mystic is reputed to have stopped the monsoon rain for five minutes to allow a friend to walk outside to a taxicab and remain dry. Once the friend was in the vehicle, the rain started up again.

Can Sai Baba really do these things? Hundreds of witnesses, in dozens of places, testify that here is a man who commands nature. But the riddle is unresolved. Physicists believe that there is an explanation, but they disagree on what it is.

Meanwhile, Sai Baba, Uri Geller, Nicholas X, and dozens of others perform inexplicable feats—and dazzled scientists scratch their heads....

Two Incredible Children

Julie Knowles is both an ordinary and an extraordinary English girl. She lives just, as they say in the south of England, "a cockstride" from the ancient stone circle of Stonehenge. She lives an even shorter distance from the mysterious village of Warminster, the quiet country town on Salisbury Plain that has catalogued more unidentified flying objects (UFO sightings) and odd happenings than could be recorded here.

Julie is fifteen years old. Dark-haired and diffident, she speaks with a slight Hampshire burr. She will talk animatedly about her "pop" music favorites, Donny and Marie Osmond, and with a certain indifference about her psychic talents.

For Julie can make objects move by mindpower alone. She can exert a physical force by nonphysical means. She is telepathic; she managed to read a talented psychic's thoughts 100 percent accurately in a transatlantic test.

Like hundreds of other children around the world, Julie had her psychic powers triggered when Uri Geller appeared on a television show

she was watching. Unlike the other children, however, Julie's abilities did not decline in the weeks following the show. She found that she was able to make a spoon or fork bend by stroking it gently, and from there she went on to develop her latent powers. She even predicted future disasters days before they happened.

Julie lives with her father, Roy, a rubber worker, in a modest home. It is Julie's brother who captures the attention; he is an extremely talented concert pianist, bright and articulate. Julie, by contrast, is shy and retiring.

Her father and brother say that Julie predicted a plane crash in Morocco days before the event and that she "saw" buildings tumbling down and people running in the streets the day before the severe earthquake in China. They add that Julie can bend spoons and make objects move. But, up to the time of my visit, these events had always happened without outside witnesses. I contacted John Hasted in London, and he arrived with his equipment.

Julie concentrated, and a strain gauge showed that, by mindpower, she had put four ounces of pressure on a brass key. Now the key was inside a glass bowl, and it was an annealed, double-screened key, chosen to prevent electrostatic effects. Drilled and with the electrodes of a strain gauge attached to it, the key was wired to a chart recorder. Julie made that key bend as it dangled in the air, and again as it lay in the bowl. Yet she never came closer to the key than eighteen inches.

Hasted set up another interesting apparatus, the sort you or I could set up at home to conduct the same experiment. He spliced together two plastic drinking straws, cut somewhat shorter than full length, into a T shape. He embedded the "foot" of the T into a flat cork and floated the cork in a saucer of water. Over the whole thing he lowered a bell-shaped glass jar.

"This is a totally nonmagnetic device," he explained. "It is under glass, so wind cannot affect it. The water ensures that vibration cannot move it a great deal either."

But Julie made it move. She concentrated fiercely. Slowly, the crosspiece of the plastic T began to rotate away from the marker he had lined up. Hasted sucked in his breath. Smoothly, the plastic straw moved, about 60 degrees. Then it stopped.

But we had seen only the beginnings of mindpower moving matter. Later, Julie went on to make the contraption rotate a full 360 degrees,

Fifteen-year-old Julie Knowles concentrates on moving a mobile made of plastic straws. Using mindpower only, she moved it an incredible 60 degrees.

*The author watches as Julie shows him
how she bends cutlery by mindpower.*

then reversed its direction at will. She bent a brass bar in a totally sealed glass tube. She bent a spoon by stroking it gently.

She also picked up a telepathic image of a horse sent by Hasted. "I've never tried telepathy before," she confessed.

I drove Julie, her father, and one of her school friends on an outing to Stonehenge. An attendant there, Bill Carnarvon, was just telling me that the ancient stone circle seemed to affect the people who worked around it, and mostly when few people were around, when Julie came up. "This is a very strange place," she said. I get odd feelings from it." Shortly after that, we left.

Back at Julie's home, I phoned my old friend Olof Jonsson, the psychic who lives in Chicago. I told him that I was interested in knowing if he could "sense" the girl's psychic abilities at long range, and I asked him if he would speak to Julie by phone. The two psychics—the young girl who just the day before had conducted her first-ever telepathy test and the Swedish engineer who once took part in successful ESP tests with an astronaut during a lunar flight—talked together for a few minutes to establish a rapport.

With the help of my shorthand notes, I can describe what happened next: Olof, in Chicago, 4,000 miles away from the quiet Wiltshire town, wrote down three images he was going to send.

Julie then told me the three images that popped into her head. "I got seven, just a number—seven. I was going to say three, but seven seemed to rub it out. Then I saw a vivid green and then there was a clock face."

I picked up the telephone. "Olof, what did you send?"

"I sent seven, green, and the image of my clock here in Chicago," the psychic chuckled. "Did she get them?"

Next, I had Julie write down three images she was going to send. She chose a fairly tall, rounded vase; a television set; and a small tomato. I rang Olof back.

He said: "I received a smooth, elongated, rounded image like a tall glass or jug. Then I got a definite square, boxy object. Last I got a red color in a circle."

By anybody's reckoning, I feel that was a fairly impressive test. It might not have been the most scientific test ever, but it totally convinced me. As far as I could see, there was no way that either person could have obtained the correct answers except by telepathy of some sort, either from each other or from me.

Julie is not the only child psychic I have met. I talked twice with ten-year-old David Shepherd at his home in Anaheim, California.

John Hasted holds a key with a strain gauge attached to it, while Julie concentrates. Julie exerted a measurable mental force on the key, as recorded on the printout of the gauge (left).

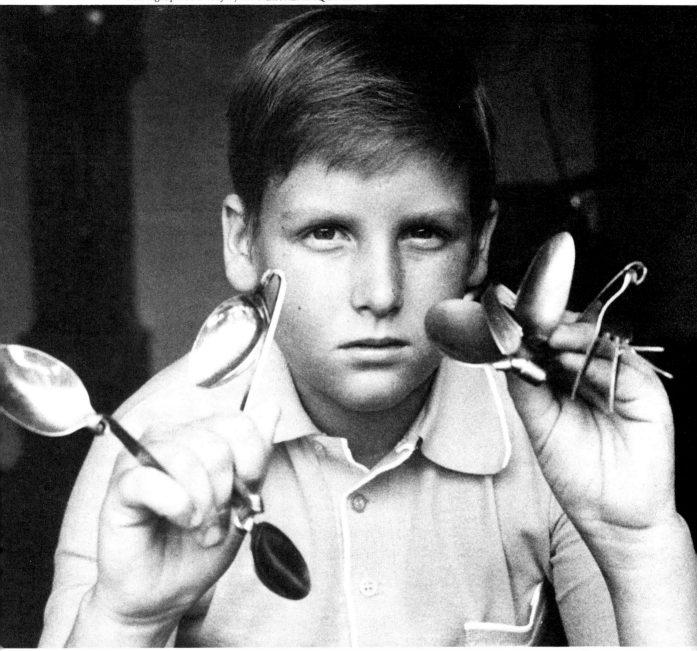

David Shepherd, a young Californian
with powers similar to those of Uri
Geller, bends metal by mindpower.

David, in a light blue paisley shirt, torn blue cord jeans, and sneakers, looked the picture of a typical American boy. But there was a difference. This ordinary boy could bend metal by mindpower, cure headaches and nervous ills, and write on a sheet of paper without touching it. The day we met, David wanted to be out playing baseball. Instead, he patiently bent spoons until he developed a headache.

Many people have read about spoon bending. Basically, the bender gently strokes a spoon. As he does so, he usually—as David did—wishes it: "Bend, bend." More often than not, the spoon will bend. David bent some spoons into a complete circle, and others into a U-shape.

I did everything I could think of to forestall any attempt at cheating. I had David wash his hands several times, before and during the test. I marked the spoons I had supplied, then checked them later to be sure that there had been no switching involved. I tasted the spoons to assure myself that no chemicals were on them. I even took them away from David to see if they could continue to bend without his aid, which they didn't.

Some people I had spoken to said that David had cured their headaches. David demurred; he insisted that spirit doctors came to effect these cures. He even pointed to a spirit doctor that he said was standing by the window. I looked, but I did not see anyone.

Other people claim that they have seen David write on a sheet of paper hidden under a carbon paper. "Usually it is a clear, sharp numeral or letter," says researcher Stewart Robb. "There is no cheating involved.

I left David with the feeling that his powers were genuine. But what produces these abilities? That is something we simply haven't quite caught up with yet....

The Bleeding Statue

Pennsylvania was the setting for another odd story. A Catholic priest, Father Henry Lovett, called me. "I believe a miracle is happening," he said. "A plaster statue of Christ is bleeding human blood."

Hundreds of pilgrims flocked to the modest Church of St. Luke, an Episcopalian parish in Eddystone, an industrial town south of Philadelphia. There, above the altar, a twenty-eight-inch-high statue of the Sacred Heart was oozing blood. A doctor confirmed that the blood was human and that it was evidently fresh as it came from the statue's hands. But under laboratory analysis, it seemed to be incredibly old.

The statue belonged to a Mrs. Ann Poore, of Lynwood. Mrs. Poore is a devout woman who had built a shrine on her front porch. Here is what she told me:

"It started the Friday after Easter. I was kneeling, praying, in the

The Reverend Chester Olszewski and Mrs. Ann Poore stand before the altar of the small church of St. Luke, Eddystone, Pennsylvania, where the statue of Christ bled.

shrine I have on my front porch. The statue was on a shelf.

"I was praying about the way people have been turning away from religion. I raised my head to look at the statue—and my heart stopped beating. I was terrified. Two rubylike drops of blood appeared over the plaster wounds in the center of each hand and started to trickle slowly down each wrist and over the red sleeve of the robe.

"I started up from my knees, astonished and in panic. It was really blood. I fell back on my knees and prayed.

"Since then, I have seen the blood flow from the statue dozens of times, and each time it has given me a deeper sense of peace, a sort of spiritual easing."

Mrs. Poore is the wife of a carpenter and the mother of five children. Her tan-colored frame home, with its lifesize statue of the Virgin in the front yard, was a place of pilgrimage before she gave the statue to the local church.

The statue itself is a perfectly ordinary commercial plaster figure. Its hands are fastened to the body by wooden dowels. During the investigations that followed the "miracle," the statue was X-rayed and the hands removed, then cemented back on. One hand was even broken, but no pipes, tubes, or mechanical trickery was found.

A sample of the blood was taken by a doctor, Joseph Rovito, and analyzed at a laboratory by a hematologist. The blood had a red-cell count only of 15 or 20 in the whole frame that was viewed—not the millions of red cells that are usually seen in fresh blood. Dr. Rovito declared that "this was human blood, undeniably, one hundred percent. I have even seen it well slowly out of the statue, while it was in St. Luke's, in my sight, twelve feet above the altar and out of anyone's reach. There was no trickery."

The statue bled for a year, causing considerable local controversy and even some religious politicking—Mrs. Poore was a Catholic and had put the statue in the hands of the local Episcopalians—when a new twist developed. Mrs. Poore developed the stigmata—the evident wounds on her hands, feet, forehead, and (she claimed) side that correspond to the wounds of the dying Christ.

I went back to Pennsylvania during the icebound winter of 1976-77, crunched through the snow to St. Luke's, and talked again with Mrs. Poore. She *did* have minor wounds. Nevertheless, I felt that she was a powerful "PK agent," a person able to induce psychokinetic effects, and the wounds were subconsciously self-induced. I was also inclined to believe that, somehow, by some mysterious ability, she had made that plaster statue bleed real blood.

I am fairly confident that she did not use crude stage-magic tech-

The statue of the Sacred Heart that bled
human blood. Before witnesses, both
hands dribbled blood "too old to date."

A close-up of the statue's blood-soaked hand. A doctor X-rayed the statue, analyzed the blood and found it human, and testified that no trickery was involved.

niques to put the blood on that statue. Some still-unproved mental ability of hers had the power to do it. But it added up to one of the more baffling stories I have covered.

One last point: Father Lovett, who carried a square of linen stained with a few drops of the blood when he visited the sick, swore that by placing the linen on the sick person, he had "never seen such peace and spiritual comfort obtained so quickly."

The Newspaper Caper

I sat with the Israeli superpsychic Uri Geller in my hotel room in Mexico City. He was about to perform a feat of mindpower that surely would have been classed as magic a couple of centuries ago. Geller, at a given time, was going to influence those of my newspaper's several million readers who cared to join in the experiment.

And he convincingly demonstrated that it worked.

The experiment was conceived a month earlier, over a luncheon with my editor at the *National Enquirer*, Ron Caylor. It was simple enough. Geller believed that if he sent out his mental powers at a given time, and if enough people "tuned him in" simultaneously, he could bend metal, restart broken watches or appliances, and cause other psychokinetic disturbances—all from a distance.

We ran Geller's picture in the *Enquirer*, with an explanatory story. We said: "At 10 P.M. EDT on Thursday, November 18, you can take part in a mind-boggling experiment." We told our readers to put spoons, broken watches, or whatever on the picture of Geller in the newspaper. Then they were to concentrate for ten or fifteen minutes. They were to will the spoon to bend, telling it, "Bend, bend." Or if a broken appliance was involved, they were to say, "Work, work."

At the same time that they were exhorting their test objects, Geller, in Mexico City, would be focusing his powers to help them achieve success. Geller explained before the experiment that the readers' minds and powers of concentration would create the energy needed to make things happen, although, or so he claimed, his psychic powers would trigger that energy.

Uri sat at a round, white table while he prepared himself. He bent my doorkey, holding it vertically, parallel to his forefinger. I watched it curl gently around to follow the curve of his fingertip. I recall thinking sourly that I might have trouble getting into my house and dissuaded him from bending any car keys on the ring. I had no wish to find myself locked out of my car.

We dragged a metal camera case across the room for Uri to put his feet on, as he insisted that he needed "more metal" to concentrate his

powers. A short while later, he felt that the experiment was complete.

After this, he did some telepathy tricks to amuse Mark Meyer, the photographer, and me. Then he left. I walked down with him to the hotel lobby. Four limousines drew quietly up in the street, his bodyguard Shipi checked the area, Geller sprinted to one of the cars, and the procession disappeared into the darkness.

Next day, Mark and I visited Geller at his hillside mansion. He was gracious and charming; he seemed to have more time to chat and exchange pleasantries.

I left for Florida vaguely dissatisfied. It had all been so undramatic. I hoped that some good results would come out of it. I expected perhaps one or two dozen readers would write and tell us what happened.

In fact, nearly 1,000 people wrote to us. About 150 of them scrawled abusive comments across the coupon the *Enquirer* article had provided for replies. But the rest reported incidents that they asserted they witnessed. And, if so, Geller's claim that he would only trigger other people's powers was accurate enough.

Some people mistook the date and did the test a week late or a week early. It seemed to make no difference. A woman from Belle Flower, Los Angeles, did it early and had three topaz rings shatter entirely on the inside, although the outside surface was unmarked.

A group of nine from Hiram, Ohio, had spoons and keys bend, watched a teapot take off, hurdle objects on the table, and fly across the room. In that same test, darts in a dartboard flew upward, out of the board.

A contractor from Pekin, Illinois, found that his broken intercom system had started working and noticed that the volume increased as he walked past it. The solenoid switches on his refrigerator "sounded like gunshots" when he walked past the appliance. The man's twelve-year-old son was scared witless when a log in the woodpile levitated and hovered in the air before tumbling back to the ground.

A rabbi from New York was called home urgently by his wife, who had watched spoons bend and move across the newspaper picture of

A bewildered Frau Barbara Scheid, of Karlstadt, Germany. During a Uri Geller TV show her silverware mysteriously began to bend without anyone being near it. Two policemen witnessed the phenomenon as knives, forks, and spoons in closed drawers snapped, twisted, and bent.

Geller. As the rabbi reached his driveway, for no accountable reason his garbage can fell over with a bang. And the strange happenings didn't end there. The electrically operated garage door started going up and down by itself—seven times in three hours.

The reports continued in this vein. Two sisters from Pasadena, Maryland, watched an aluminum key snap into two pieces. A freelance artist from Hattiesburg, Mississippi looked on in awe as a table knife slid from its position about six or eight inches—five times. Around the country, Christmas tree lights that were not even plugged in lit up; several people claimed cures of long-standing illnesses; surgical tweezers, scissors, a steel knife sharpener, and steel keys all bent.

One experimenter used a dead battery. He first had it checked by a jeweler at 0.2 volts. After the experiment, it read 1.65 volts, which is more than the normal range for a new battery. And broken watches were a favorite target; many of the successful experimenters reported that their watches had restarted.

Could all these people be lying? I spoke to many of them on the phone after the event, and I do not think they could all be phony.

About Uri Geller

The Geller phenomenon is too well documented to ignore. But what is it? Geller himself believes: "The people who experienced these phenomena have the power stronger in them than other people do—but everybody has it."

Children seem to have "the power" to a conspicuous degree. In Europe, Geller has appeared on television in several countries, and many children have been discovered with psychic abilities. Like David Shepherd of Los Angeles, who discovered his ability after attending a psychic fair and seeing pictures of the phenomenon, these children simply needed to have their imaginations opened to the possibility.

After Geller's TV shows in Italy and Switzerland, so many children turned up with psychic ability that researchers started calling them *Gellerini*, or mini-Gellers. A New York parapsychologist, James Hickman, was walking with a mini-Geller in the park. On her wrist was a broken watch, which Hickman was observing carefully, for he expected it to restart. He was holding the girl's hand, and as the watch was strapped to that same wrist, it would have been difficult for her to tamper with it without Hickman's knowledge.

Uri Geller (left) pauses for the cameraman on a sidewalk in Mexico City. With Geller is his bodyguard-assistant, Shipi.

Suddenly, the watch was no longer there. Hickman and the girl searched for it without success and returned to his apartment. Hickman went directly to the refrigerator for a cold drink. Inside was the missing watch—and it was very cold, as if it had been there for some time.

A good friend of mine, an engineer and scientist whose word I trust implicitly, worked with Geller on some of the early experiments in California. One day he left the apartment where Geller and his group were working, unlocked his car, closed the door, and sat there astonished. Two wine bottles of a very distinctive shape had dropped onto the seat alongside him. They were the bottles from which the group in the apartment had been drinking.

Others also attest to Geller's odd powers. John Taylor, professor of applied mathematics at King's College, University of London, is the author of numerous scientific papers and was recently voted one of the world's top twenty scientists by *New Scientist* magazine. Here is what Taylor had to say:

"Yes, odd things happened to me when I was testing Uri Geller. We were in the laboratory at my college. Only the two of us were in the room, and I was monitoring Uri during a metal-bending exercise. Suddenly, only a second or two after I had noticed a two-inch strip of copper in its place at one end of the laboratory, I glimpsed it flying the length of the lab—about thirty feet—before it fell to the floor near the doorway. The door was closed.

"I was shaken, but carried on working. The metal was at the opposite end of the room, where it had fallen. Five minutes later, I heard a 'clunk' and looked up to see that it had disappeared from where it had landed before.

"Uri remarked that it would never turn up again, implying that the metal had dematerialized forever. He was quite matter-of-fact about it. But after he left the laboratory, I carried out a careful search and found the metal under a radiator, in a place into which it could hardly have been thrown. Besides, there was no method I could see that could have caused the metal to be moved physically by Uri. He was never nearer than ten feet to it, and I was closely watching him for my own monitoring purposes."

The dark-haired scientist paused, then continued: On another occasion a plastic tube with a piece of wire embedded in it—so that it could not be bent manually—flew about twenty feet without anyone being near it. When I examined the wire, it had a ten-degree bend in it—yet the plastic was unmarked.

"On yet a third occasion, a five-inch piece of aluminum flew the length of the laboratory when nobody was near it."

John Taylor looked around his brightly lit office off London's

Strand and said soberly: "I am convinced there was no trickery. Neither was it a fanciful flight of imagination. These were paranormal events."

Any number of scientific researchers have tested Geller extensively and witnessed all kinds of phenomena and thousands of people in audiences across the world have seen him perform. They all believe Geller has amazing powers. But many people do not think so. They consider Geller to be nothing more than a sophisticated stage magician.

My view lies somewhere between these two extremes. I think Geller *does* have paranormal abilities. But Uri Geller, likable, outgoing and talented as he is, is still a showman. He revels in the dramatic, and this is bound to make people somewhat suspicious of him.

Geller's first major scientific investigation in the United States was held at the Stanford Research Institute and conducted by the team of Harold Puthoff and Russell Targ, two innovative young physicists. They spent six weeks with Uri Geller. All kinds of phenomena followed them about but, sadly for the scientists, they felt that although they witnessed these phenomena, none of them were performed under sufficiently controlled conditions for an unequivocal "Well, that proves *that.*" Here are some of the strange happenings:

A brand-new and unopened deck of cards was provided by Russell Targ. He handed the cards to Geller, who shuffled them, then dropped them onto a tabletop. The cards appeared to penetrate the table. On examination, five of the cards were found to have a missing diagonal slice.

Geller spent one evening bending spoons, rings, and other metal objects. When Drs. Puthoff and Targ left his apartment, they found that a stop sign at the end of the driveway had been bent into three complete loops during their nighttime metal-bending session. Coincidence? Someone using heavy machinery?

On another occasion, as Geller and the two researchers were going to lunch, the trio saw people working around a TV monitor. A sound-wave system, somewhat like an X-ray, was being tested. Geller held up his fist and shouted: "Up, down, up, down." The image on the monitor obeyed him.

Another time, when the scientists were attempting to get Geller to move a light beam by mindpower, he simply opted to move the pen of the chart recorder. He shouted: "Move!" The pen moved all the way across the paper and never moved again. The preamplifiers of the recorder's two channels were burned out and had to be changed.

"We just do not know the whole answer," admitted Targ. "But we do know that working with Geller allowed us to observe some very unusual events."

Life and Death— or is it?

Psychic Medicine

Robert Leichtman is a physician who discovered while practicing in California that he possesses an unusual talent.

"I know it sounds incredible," he confessed, "but I can go into the minds of people and sense what is causing their ailments. I need no information about them other than name, address, and sex. I don't need to see or contact them. These days, I usually work as a consultant for psychiatrists who need more information about their patients."

Fantastic? I thought so. So I talked to Norman Shealy, clinical associate professor of neurosurgery at two northern universities. Dr. Shealy said: "I tested Dr. Leichtman by sending him the names, sexes, ages, and addresses of twenty-five patients whose mental states I was knowledgable about. Within a few days I had back typewritten reports on them, giving me details of their mental makeup, frustrations, innermost secret feelings and resentments. Dr. Leichtman also told me the site, nature, and cause of their ailments.

"When I compared his analyses with the ones I had done, using a standard psychological analysis that takes hours per patient to conduct and assess, I found that he was at least 92 percent accurate, and possibly 96 percent."

Dr. Shealy was so impressed that he conducted another test—and Dr. Leichtman scored 98 percent accurate. "He was even able to tell me the specific causes of three paraplegics' injuries, down to saying that one girl was crippled because of a self-inflicted gunshot wound—and he was exactly right."

Dr. Leichtman now lives in the northeastern part of the United

Olga Worrall, faith healer extraordinary.

Robert Leichtman, M.D., dictates his thoughts aloud as he meditates on a patient's ills. His in-the-mind explanations of root causes of physical ailments have helped cure hundreds of sick people.

States and works with several psychiatrists, all of whom gave me glowing reports about him. One said: "In a case of multiple personality, Dr. Leichtman quickly established that it was a genuine case of demoniac possession. I had a priest perform an exorcism, and the patient was cured immediately. Interestingly, we even identified the demon— a girl whom we established had died of a drug overdose in New York."

From psychic diagnosis to psychic healing is a short step, and America, like my native England, has its fair share of psychic healers. Probably the most famous is Baltimore's Olga Worrall. More than three hundred people attend her healing clinic each week, and scores of documented healings attest to her abilities.

Most skeptics counter the claim that healers are responsible for curing their patients by saying, "There probably wasn't anything really wrong with the person in the first place—it was all psychosomatic." But Mrs. Worrall, a warm, grandmotherly woman, has proved her abilities time and again. Researchers have discovered mysterious forces that come from her hands, energy capable of altering the hydrogen bonding of water, of affecting a cloud chamber (a laboratory device to trace subatomic particles), and of making dramatic "flares" on pictures taken with high-voltage photographic techniques. She has even affected "sick" enzymes—living organisms—and made them better. It's not easy to play psychological games with primitive life forms.

One clue to her success might have come out of some of her work. Edward Brame, a researcher who works on water analysis by measuring its infrared light properties, said: "After Mrs. Worrall concentrated over a sealed flask of water, its properties were changed and it was somehow energized. In tests with this energized water, we found that it helped people heal faster. It also made plants grow up to eight times quicker. Interestingly, similar results were obtained from water that had been prayed over by a prayer group in Georgia."

Could this be the secret meaning of the "Fountain of Youth"? It's another riddle that scientists are scratching their heads over. But there are even more strange happenings going on in our world....

The Spirit Doctors

It was cold, and specks of snow slanted past me as I stood in picture-postcard surroundings seventy miles south of the Arctic Circle, in Iceland. With photographer John Miller and an interpreter, I had journeyed to a remote mountain farm—*Einarsstadir*, literally "Einar's farm"—to speak with the man everyone in Iceland knows as Einar the Healer.

Psychic healer Einar Jonsson, a sheep rancher from northern Iceland, stands at the edge of his land. Behind him is the farmhouse and private church built by his family. Einarstaddir has been his family's home for over a thousand years.

Jonsson looks over some of the voluminous mail he receives each week, much of it pleas for help from his spirit doctors.

It was a long and difficult trek from the sunshine of Florida, a trek that had already cost John and me some anxious moments when we drowned our four-wheel-drive vehicle in a glacier-fed river. But the welcome we received from Einar Jonsson was warm enough to make us forget it.

We walked into Einar's cozy farmhouse, a home heated by piped steam from a nearby hot spring, and were greeted with impressions of well-scrubbed wooden furniture, the smell of baking bread, and dazzling white linen. Outside, above the red roof and white walls of the sheep ranch, the snowy flanks of Fljotšheidi Mountain had risen protectively. Gray, brown, and black sheep had grazed on the gentle folds of the valley sides; among them, Einar had proudly pointed out Bjorisson, his prize ram.

Einar, a weathered, seamed gnome of a man, with the hard hands of a rancher, is famous for feats of healing. We had come to hear from him about his uncanny powers that can produce such cures. He has helped countless people and journeys five hundred miles across the ice and lava fields to heal the sick in Reykjavik, the nation's capital, several times a year. University researchers have asked to test his powers, but he says he cannot spare the time.

An average healing session takes twenty minutes, but some may go on for four hours. Einar claims no credit for his healings. "I have spirit doctors who do cures through me," he explained. "The chief one is Thordur Palsson, a doctor from Organes, a small town in the west of Iceland. He died in 1920. I also have other spirit guides who do healing, but I did not know of this ability until I attended a seance in 1956.

"Today, people come to see me all the time. I ask the spirit doctors to heal them. Sometimes I even ask the doctors to heal animals. I write down the name and address of the patient, and the doctors tell me what to say or do. Usually I put my hand on the patient's hands and that is enough of a bridge for the spirit doctors to heal them."

Einar has gray hair that is receding, blue eyes, and strong square hands. He moves his shoulders inside the gray and brown wool sweater knitted for him by his wife Erla, from wool taken from his own sheep. His eyes fill with tears as he speaks of his most incredible case:

"My stepdaughter, Gunna, was in a car wreck. She had brain damage, crushed kidneys; her ribcage was almost totally destroyed. Her spine was displaced. The doctors told my wife, who was with her in Reykjavik, five hundred miles away, that she would be a vegetable at best—if she lived."

"I pleaded with Einar," recalls Erla, his beautiful blonde wife. "I asked him to ask his spirit doctors to help."

And, from hundreds of miles away, Einar sent out his healing forces.

"Gunna," whose right name is Gudrun but who is always known by her pet name, knew nothing of it. Yet, within a few days she was alert, happy, and getting better. She left the hospital after a week; the body that was so badly broken had repaired itself. Today Gudrun has completely recovered.

"I knew I was dying," she says, "then I felt someone kind and caring was working to help me. I felt a great sense of relief. I knew instantly that I would not die, that a mysterious force was going to keep me alive and make me better. I know now it was Einar's spirit doctor who was making me well. And since that accident I have never had any illness. I feel wonderful. Every single day of my life has a new and special meaning."

"Hers was an amazing case," Ulfur Ragnarsson, Gudrun's doctor, told me. "It convinced me that Einar has paranormal powers. The girl had a ribcage almost totally destroyed, punctured lungs, brain damage of the worst kind, and she was virtually crippled from displacement of the spine. Her kidneys were crushed, and we put her into an iron lung because of her lung damage. She had suffered massive concussion and cerebral hemorrhaging. I was convinced that if she did survive, it would be as a cripple and an idiot. Yet her ribcage mysteriously repaired itself; and today she has no other damage. She even walked out of the hospital within a week."

Einar can cite countless other examples of his spirit doctors' work. He cured a four-year-old boy of stunted hands—hands that were frostbitten when the child was two—that medical science had given up as hopeless. Einar held the child's hands for half an hour. Today, although the hands are still not quite normal, they are growing. The afflicted boy, Leifur Ingolfsson, can use them—as he could within three days of the uncanny treatment.

"It was a miracle," exclaims the boy's father. "My son had seen the best specialists in Iceland, and for two years they could do nothing. Then, days after Einar had worked on his hands, they were back in use again."

I checked on other stories of cures—of stroke victims and people

This pretty Reykjavik girl, Gudrun Sverirsdottir, believes she owes her life to the intervention of spirit doctors on her behalf. Against all medical odds, she is today completely healed from a near-fatal auto accident.

with cataracts, of heart disease victims and arthritis sufferers. All of them seemed genuine. The minister who arranges Einar's free healing services in Reykjavik testified to hundreds of cases of healings. I could only wonder, What force causes these strange happenings?

Glimpses of the Afterlife

Scientists are amassing evidence that may someday prove an afterlife. Recent research has unearthed cases of incredible similarity from around the world, and these similarities may provide the necessary clues to "prove" the survival of consciousness. Perhaps the most convincing evidence to date comes from an American thanatologist, an expert on dying, Elisabeth Kübler-Ross.

Dr. Kübler-Ross is now fifty years old. Swiss by birth, she is a former assistant professor of psychiatry at the University of Chicago and is the leading researcher on death and dying in the world. She has spent seven years collecting information from terminally ill patients. I had to interview her on a plane flight to Chicago, so crowded is her work schedule.

"I am totally convinced of life after death," she told me, "because I have seen about one thousand of my patients die. Some have been clinically dead and have revived to describe what they saw; others have described their first glimpses of the next life.

"Even little children of two, three, and four years old report things similar things to those that adults experience. I believe that everyone who dies experiences these things: they are met by loved ones; they become physically whole again, for example, an amputated leg will be restored; they float out of their bodies; they feel a sense of great peace and beauty. And many who have been declared dead and have been revived did not want to come back.

"Many people who have been clinically dead—and some of the patients I talked with have been dead for as long as six and one half hours before being revived—reported that they were 'sent back' or told, 'Your time has not yet come.'

"One little boy of two died clinically for about an hour, then was revived. He said that he had been met by Mary and Jesus—both his parents were alive, by the way—and that they had told him to go back, because the time was not right.

"He said he wanted to stay, so Mary told him: 'You must go back

Dr. Elisabeth Kübler-Ross, author of On Death and Dying. *Her research on deathbed experiences has expanded the consciousness of scientists.*

now to save Mummy from the fire.' The child's mother was very upset to hear this, thinking that she was regarded as sinful, until she blurted out: 'If he had died, I would have gone through Hell.' Then she realized what was the 'fire' her child's revival had saved her from."

Dr. Kübler-Ross, who has several children of her own, related a case of a twelve-year-old girl who died and was revived. "She told her father, whom she loved dearly, 'I was met by my brother and by a sense of incredible love. I didn't want to come back, but they sent me.' Then she added, 'It was wonderful, but I don't have a dead brother, do I? And that was when both parents broke down and cried. The girl did have a dead brother, but she had not known about him."

Dr. Kübler-Ross endured years of ridicule from professional groups before they recognized the value of her work. She investigated cases that illustrated facets of death and dying that few people know about.

"It seems that in time of great bodily pain or fear, the soul goes out of body and calmly, dispassionately, witnesses what is happening to the body it just left," the doctor explained. "One patient described to me the auto accident he was in, when he 'saw' his amputated leg lying, out of his sight, in the roadway. And he told about rescuers' sympathy and actions he couldn't physically see because he was trapped in his car. Yet he knew about them because he was 'floating' over the accident scene."

Another revived patient, who had 'died' on the operating table, told how she and a dead friend watched the operation being conducted below them on her earthly body. Although she was under deep anesthesia during her operation, she later described a surgical error that needed repairing, told of things she could not have seen from the operating table, and recounted to the surgeon large portions of his conversation during the time she was clinically dead.

Another uncanny consistency throughout the stories concerns the dying person being met by loved ones. Says Dr. Kübler-Ross: "I ask my dying children, 'Who would you most like to take with you when you die?' Ninety-nine percent of them say Mummy or Daddy. Yet none of them with living parents have ever reported seeing Mummy or Daddy waiting for them as they die. Usually, it is a spirit guide or guardian angel. Sometimes it is Jesus or Mary. Never is it Mummy or Daddy, if the parents are alive. Yet that is who the child wants to see. The rule seems to be: the person you love most who is already dead waits to help you. You are never alone when you die."

Much the same findings were reported by Karlis Osis, research fellow of the American Society for Psychical Research. The Society received $1 million from the estate of an Arizona miner, James Kidd, who specified that his money go to the best-qualified group that would attempt to prove the existence of a soul and life after death. The legacy has now run out, but the researchers did uncover some fascinating evidence for an afterlife with the funds.

Dr. Osis talked to me in his Manhattan office. "I have seen too much evidence for life after death to ignore the facts," he said. "I have made extensive studies involving deathbed observations by doctors and nurses in India and America. I gathered hundreds of eyewitness accounts from medical staffs. And time after time, it was reported that shortly before death, apparitions of friends or relatives came to the dying person. They seemed to be coming to take the patient away to another existence. Usually, patients who saw apparitions tended to die within an hour or so, but after seeing the apparitions, the patients invariably seemed much calmer, and death was made easier."

Dr. Osis approached the question of life after death from another angle. He believes that "if we can successfully demonstrate that the soul has a separate life, apart from the brain, that could be major evidence." This belief led him to investigate astral travel—out-of-body experiences.

"In one case I investigated carefully, in India," he relates, "a holy man was visiting a family and went into their prayer room for half an hour. During that time, he appeared to a group of people four hundred miles away, people who knew him well. He mentioned it to the family when he came out of their prayer room, and I was able to substantiate his claim. There was no question that an imposter had been involved at either site.

"In my own work here in New York, I was once testing a psychic, Claudette Kiely, of Massachusetts, for out-of-body experiences. She was to 'fly in' to my office at a given time and view a target, a white X, although she did not know what the target was."

For this experiment, Dr. Osis had observers in the room. At the agreed time, some mysterious blue smoke materialized out of thin air directly over the target X.

The observers reported it as "simply a spiral of blue smoke that seemed to materialize, then dematerialize." Later, the psychic accurately described the target, and she mentioned that she had seen herself flying over an industrial landscape and at one point had flown directly through a thick column of smoke belching out of a factory chimney. The time coincided exactly with the appearance of the smoke in Dr. Osis's office.

Everybody has heard stories of contact with the dead, and these often occur in dreams. One of the most famous cases of communication with the dead concerns Mr. Chaffin's will.

Mr. Chaffin was a wealthy North Carolinian and the father of four sons. In a fit of irritation with them, he cut three of his sons out of his will. Soon after he made his new will, he died. The will was uncontested, but the son who received the whole estate kept having dreams about his father. In one of them the father appeared, in an agitated state, wearing his favorite overcoat. He kept pointing to the inside pocket and referring to a particular verse from the Bible.

The son awoke, very much shaken, and went to a hall closet, which still held some of his father's clothes. He found the overcoat, with the Bible in its inside pocket. He turned to the verse and found a new, witnessed will that had been made shortly before his father's death, reinstating the other three sons as beneficiaries.

The new will went to probate and was found genuine.

An equally astonishing case of communication from the grave involved Erlendur Haraldsson, a professor of psychology in Iceland. He related how six years of investigating this case convinced him that it was genuine. In the course of his research, he checked twenty specific points the dead man had made and found only one of them doubtful. Here is Haraldsson's story:

In September 1940, a young truck driver, Gudni Magnusson, was driving from Reydarfjordur to Eskifjordur, a long and strenuous journey. He ran out of gasoline, walked four miles to a gas station, walked back to his car, and finally drove home. But he was exhausted. He developed severe stomach pains, and the next day two doctors decided to move him to a hospital. But it was late in the evening and they could not get an airplane. Instead, they tried to move Gudni by motorboat. He died enroute to the hospital.

Months later, at a séance, psychic Hafsteinn Bjornsson kept being interrupted by a spirit communicator. Questions revealed that the communicator was Gudni. He named names, cited places, and told how he had been stretching out under his truck to see what was wrong with it when he had ruptured a spot in his intestines that had been weakened by surgery in childhood.

Almost every detail of Gudni's story checked out. Haraldsson was able to confirm all that he related except that the spirit claimed to know members of the family of one of the séance sitters. They were not aware of any personal connection.

"It is certainly a case of paranormal functioning," Haraldsson told me.

But it was not the most amazing part of the story. The psychic who communicated with Gudni is sixty-year-old Hafsteinn Bjornsson. He is a small, silver-haired man who works in the bill collection department of the state radio station in Reykjavik. Bjornsson is famous across Iceland for his psychic powers. In laboratory tests, he has shown astounding accuracy in naming dead people connected with test subjects unknown to him and whom he could not even see. Sometimes he was able to describe how the people died and their physical characteristics. His most amazing experiment involved a ghost who came back to get his severed leg buried properly.

Bjornsson was at a séance where a spirit identifying himself as Runolfur Runolfsson—Runki, for short—was the communicator. Runki told how he had died at fifty-two when he sat down drunk on the beach, fell asleep, and was washed away. He cited where and when it happened and grumbled that when his body was swept ashore, dogs and ravens had torn it apart. His thighbone was swept out to sea, then washed ashore later.

The ghost complained: "It is now in Ludvik's house."

Erlendur Haraldsson, who set about finding out what had happened, reports: "In fact, a carpenter building a wall at that house had actually put the femur of a very tall man between the inner and outer walls. He didn't want to throw it away disrespectfully, and it couldn't be buried in the churchyard without knowing whose it was, so he disposed of it that way."

The séance group that located the carpenter's hiding place buried the bone and held a short service. The psychic Bjornsson did not go to the "funeral," but at a séance that same day, he communicated with Runki. The ghost thanked the people for the service, described who was there, even named the different cakes served at the clergyman's home, and thanked especially the couple who had arranged it all!

Reincarnation

The famous Washington seer Jeane Dixon was convinced of the fact of reincarnation after a series of startlingly vivid dreams she had in 1976 showed her glimpses of her own previous lives. She saw herself as a Tibetan monk who specialized in healing, as an Aztec who watched in horror as prisoners were slaughtered, as an Asian peasant who was killed by the soldiers of Gehghis Khan, and as an Egyptian astronomer who saw slaves building a pyramid.

In her incarnation as the astronomer, she dreamed in such detail that "I seemed to smell the very dust in the air. I heard the chanting songs of hundreds of slaves as they heaved great blocks of sandstone into position and I felt the heat of the sun on my face. I was wearing a robe of stiff linen and I had in my hand a roll of heavy parchment or papyrus."

Mrs. Dixon, slight and elegant in a navy two-piece suit, fingered

Washington seer Jeane Dixon believes that in a previous life she was an Egyptian astronomer.

the gold and amethyst-studded crucifix she wears around her neck. She recalled her dream of life as a Tibetan monk. "I saw myself leaving the stone monastery, which clung precariously to the side of a cliff, like the nest of some giant bird, to travel to the east, to the lowlands and valleys. I remember flat-roofed houses, red and white. The monastery seemed to have opaque windows, not glass, and no protection from the bitter cold. There were monastery dogs, black mastiffs. I remember the scent of burning incense, crowded jostling monks at mealtimes.

"When monks died, their bodies were usually put in a special place where the vultures came. I remember seeing those horrible black birds fluttering over my body while I seemed to float above it, watching dispassionately. Only my eternal spirit was valuable."

Is there such a thing as reincarnation? Who knows? Cases investigated in India describe children knowing people they have never met before, and these children are able to describe places they have never visited. An American from the Midwest is convinced that he was once a monk in northern England. He compiled a list of some two hundred points of information and went to the abbey where he believes he once lived. Many of his points checked out, but I felt that none of them was conclusive.

Fredrick Davies, an English palmist who now lives in New York, examined the hands of Jeane Dixon. Jeane has incredibly old-looking palms, incongruously so, and they are crossed with hundreds of lines and wrinkles, including a perfect six-pointed star. This, Davies assured me, is the Star of Prophecy.

"These lines tell me indisputably that Jeane has lived many lives, that she has a very ancient spirit," he declared.

But is that evidence of reincarnation? I simply do not know.

Perhaps the last word on the subject should go to Jeane Dixon. She once predicted: "One day we shall understand the secrets of reincarnation. All the accumulated knowledge of dozens of previous lives which is stored, locked away, in our minds, will be released. Our brains will become like giant computers, heavy with knowledge. We shall be equipped to solve all our problems—of war, famine, and disease."

OUT THERE

Ancient legends from North Africa, Australia, and the remote mountains of Central and South America all tell the story of gods who came from the skies. The Swiss researcher-author Erich von Daniken wrote a best-selling book *Chariots of the Gods?* and attracted a decade of both acclaim and acrimony. Let's see what you think about it.

Consider these points:

- An American scholar believes that these ancient gods were half fish and half men and that they left incredible knowledge of the universe that is still preserved by a primitive African tribe.
- An ancient Indian temple seems to have a band of radiation of exact, straight-line dimensions running 170 feet to its high altar—a band that some researchers think was a guide beam for spacecraft.
- In South America, incredibly carved stones picture sophisticated medical techniques and an ancient Aztec peering at the stars through a telescope.
- Cave paintings in remote mountains of the Baja show an uncanny resemblance to similar paintings in Australia and Africa. They portray space-helmeted men with antennae; one even shows a space vehicle with flames from its underside.
- Other cave paintings, known to be hundreds of years old, show genetic engineering techniques first discovered in 1956.
- A British astronomer believes that he has decoded signals from an alien space probe that has been circling the earth for 13,000 years.

Are these things evidence of visitors from space? If you want to investigate further, consider these points:

- A Cornell University professor of astronomy, Carl Sagan, suggests that there could be one million civilizations in our galaxy alone.

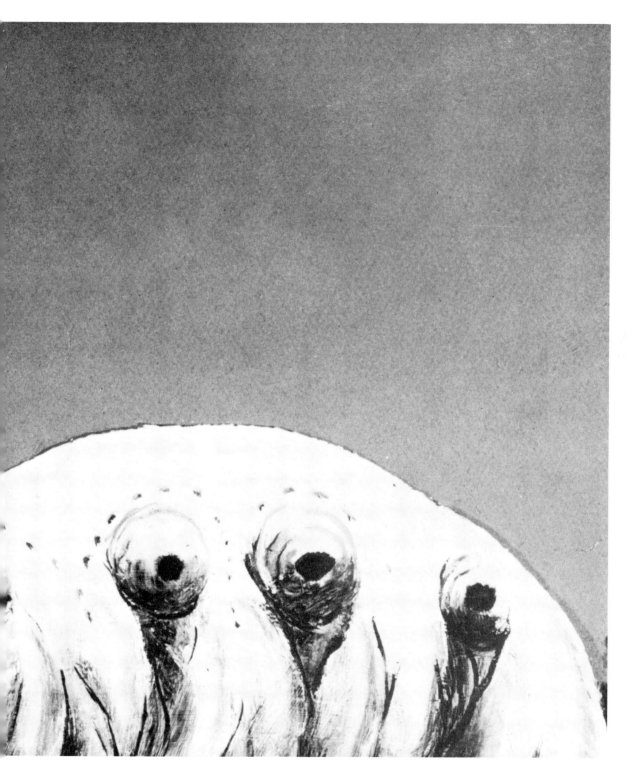

What's Out There? Monsters we might meet include this multilegged Bandersnatch, a grass-grazer that would weigh 30,000 pounds on a high-gravity planet.

How about this Great Filter Bat, a tropical resident of a high-gravity planet and an insect-eater weighing 150 pounds?

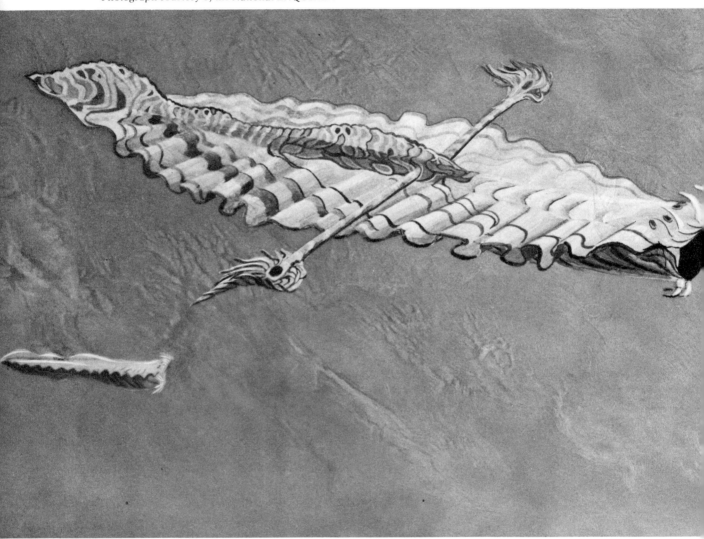

Or perhaps this cold-climate, filter-feeding carnivore called the Outrigger Ribbons Fish with armlike projections that are sensitive to the touch of its prey?

- Nobel prizewinner George Wald, of Harvard, thinks that contact with another civilization would be "a nightmare."
- UFO experts are increasingly concerned at the ever more frequent reports of callous, almost brutal treatment of UFO victims—by the aliens themselves.
- A new mystery is emerging from UFO reports, of strange "men in black" who terrorize witnesses to UFO sightings long after the event. And the accounts agree on one thing: the "men in black" do not seem to be human.

What then, is Out There?

The Godlike
Fish-Men of Dogon

Robert Temple is a man of considerable academic standing. A fellow of the prestigious Royal Astronomical Society, London, the thirty-one-year-old researcher from the University of Pennsylvania spent nine years tracing an amazing trail of clues across Africa.

Says Temple: "Half-man-half-fish aliens from space brought civilization to the ancient world. I think that travelers from the star system Sirius, mammals like dolphins with the bodies of men and the tails of fish, visited Earth between five and ten thousand years ago."

Today, memories of those long-gone star travelers are preserved in some startling knowledge possessed by the Dogon, a primitive tribe from Mali, on the edge of the Sahara Desert. For the Dogon worship an invisible star—that is really there. They know exact details of its orbital timings. They even drew its elliptical orbit hundreds of years before astronomers knew that an elliptical orbit was possible. They know, too, that their sacred star is incredibly small and heavy and that it is made of a "special," unearthly material.

In every way, the Dogon appear to be correct. The latest knowledge in astronomy supports the primitive tribe's beliefs. Sirius B is a white dwarf star, incredibly dense. It is invisible to the naked eye and to most telescopes because the light of Sirius obscures it. In fact, Sirius B was not even discovered until 1865, nor photographed until 1970.

Temple, who studied Sanskrit, the ancient language of India, to help him in his research, discovered that the Dogon knew of a landing by a rocketlike craft and mentioned a "mother craft" that hovered over it. And, in the incredibly preserved legends, which describe Sirius B as the home of their gods, Temple even found descriptions of those gods.

"They were half man, half fish," he told me. "They were like dolphins with a mouth and separate blowhole for breathing. Dogon tradition reveals that these blowholes were two long, thin slits below the collarbone.

Dr. Robert Temple, shown here in his office in England, is the researcher who solved the mystery of the Dogon tribe's knowledge.

"I'm convinced that the Dogon are descendants of ancient Egyptian or Babylonian tribes. I think that when these travelers from Sirius came to Earth they made contact with the highest form of civilization they could find—the Egyptians or Babylonians—not some obscure desert tribe. Ironically, it was the desert tribe that preserved the information!"

I asked one of the world's leading authorities on the Dogon, British anthropologist Francis Huxley, about the legends. Huxley has spent ten years studying the Dogon and believes they have an extraordinary mathematical and philosophical culture for a primitive people.

"There is something deeply mysterious and disturbing about these facts" he admitted. "It could well be that they are memories of contact with another world."

Photograph courtesy of the United States Naval Observatory.

The first photograph ever taken of the mysterious Sirius B—the tiny star to the lower right of the star Sirius. The other "dots" in the photo are small multiple images of Sirius itself.

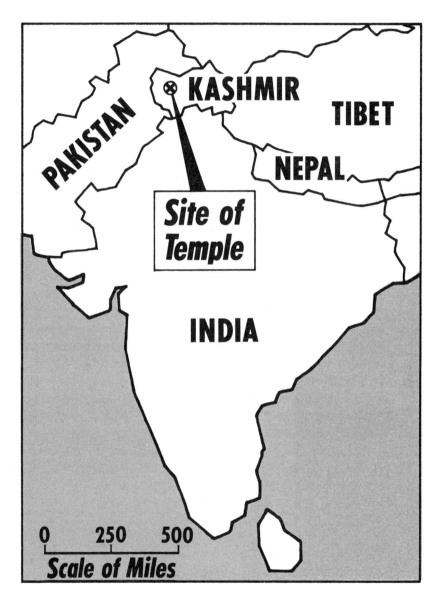

Site of the Temple of the Sun at Martand,
in the foothills of the Himalayas, where
Erich von Daniken found a mysterious
line of radiation.

Ezekiel's Temple

More tangible mementoes of an alien contact can be found in the hot, dusty foothills of the Himalayas, in Kashmir, claims author-researcher Erich von Daniken.

I met von Daniken, who is forty-two years of age, in the elegant dining room of Zurich's Eden au Lac hotel. In a matter-of-fact-manner he related how he had recently returned from an expedition to Kashmir to track down biblical references that he decided were accounts of spacecraft landings. He explained what had started him on his quest:

"Ezekiel was taken by 'God' to a temple. He described a man 'like brass' and the approach of 'the glory of God' with a noise like many waters. This, I think, was a description of a spaceman and the approach of a spaceship. Ezekiel, who was shown the land from a high place—probably a viewing platform of the spacecraft—described in great detail the way priests of the temple must dress, probably to counteract radioactivity."

On this slender evidence, the muscular, dark-haired von Daniken equipped an expedition and went to Kashmir, in northern India. Why Kashmir? In answer, von Daniken drove me to the Alps above Zurich to his home, to see the results of his search.

His living room was crowded with souvenirs of exotic lands —carved stone figures from Peru and Bolivia, Indian brass and silver, Persian hangings, and Hopi medicine-man dolls. Downstairs, in his library, the walls were covered with filing drawers, indexes, and charts. Books on subjects as diverse as Inca ceremonial ritual and NASA spacecraft propulsion reports stood side by side.

Von Daniken took out a thick manila folder of photographs and charts. He said, "Josef Blumrich, a friend of mine who was once head of spacecraft design at NASA, wrote a book about Ezekiel's descriptions of God's craft, and pointed out that it was a description, in nontechnical language, of an advanced spacecraft. In biblical chapters forty to forty-seven of Ezekiel, there is an account of how the prophet was taken by God to a place and told to write down what he saw."

According to von Daniken, Ezekiel was taken to a spacecraft repair shop. Later, the spot was considered holy and a temple was erected on the site. Von Daniken decided that the Temple of the Sun at Martand, some twenty miles southeast of Srinagar, was the most probable site. The Temple at Martand best matched Ezekiel's fairly obscure description. It faced the correct point of the compass, and was located in the high place above a river valley that Ezekiel had mentioned. The temple's age and general layout fit in with Ezekiel's description. Details of architecture—notably distinctive water drainage pipes running under the walls—were also correct.

Author-researcher von Daniken holds a
photograph of the Martand temple.

Von Daniken's assistant, Willi Dunenberger, uses a geiger counter to locate
traces of radiation.

F. M. Hassnain, the Indian scholar whose researches in Kashmir have been concerned with legends of gods from the sky.

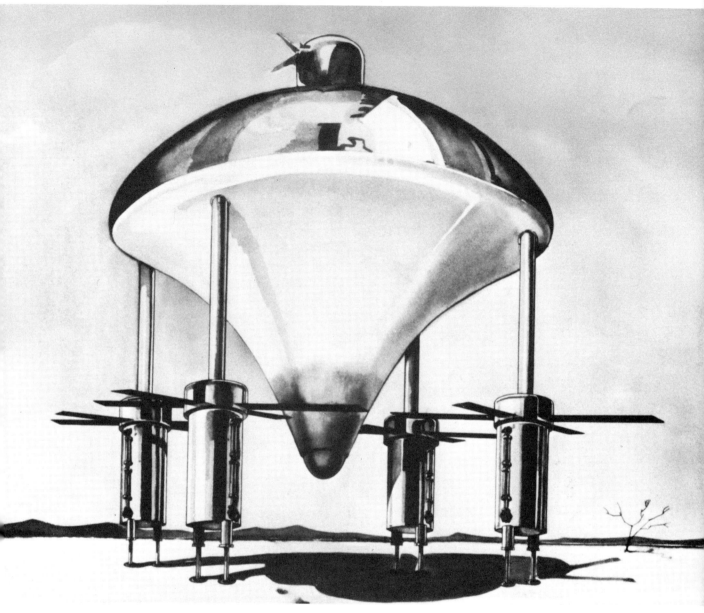

Ezekiel's fiery chariot? Josef F. Blumrich of the Marshall Space Flight Center, Huntsville, Alabama, agrees with von Daniken's theory that Ezekiel's chariot was an atomic-powered atmospheric-entry vehicle with four helicopterlike "dinghies" for local transportation on planets it visited.

At the temple, measurements revealed a dead-straight line of radiation. "The needle went off the gauge," recalls von Daniken's research assistant, Willi Dunenberger. The band of radiation stretched 52 meters long and 1.5 meters wide, from temple gate to high altar. "It was probably left there after spacecraft workshop activity at the site," comments Dr. Blumrich.

"It could be an invisible signpost, with some message for us," speculated von Daniken. "Someday we might solve the riddle."

A local researcher, F.M. Hassnain of Srinagar, accompanied von Daniken and witnessed the startling readings of the geiger counter. "The evidence is amazing," he said. "There is a clear and unnaturally straight band of radioactivity running all the way from the main gate to the stone altar, and there seems to be something metallic buried deep inside the altar.

"I am a researcher in Hindu writings and folklore that tell of Hindu astronauts three million years ago. There are many references to astronauts in ancient Kashmir. I am hoping to be able to obtain a permit to dig at the temple and find out exactly what is the cause of this unnatural radioactivity."

And there the mystery rests ... for now.

The Astronauts of Peru

In Ica, Peru, another legend of ancient astronauts is waiting to be resolved. Ica is a town of some 50,000 population and lies south of Lima. Jose Cabrera, a professor of anthropology and history, has carved evidence that he believes shows that visitors from the stars visited the Peruvian natives 30,000 years ago. For Dr. Cabrera has collected some 14,000 carved stones. These show heart transplants, using modern surgical techniques; Caesarean-section births; brain transplants and surgery; star maps, with Indians using telescopes; and aerial views of North and South America. Stones that show surgical techniques show blood vessels, surgeons with cutting instruments, and patients with tubes running from their mouths, like some life-support system.

Former NASA Spacecraft designer Josef Blumrich has seen these stones and has made microscopic analyses of the grooves in them. His conclusion: they are tens of thousands of years old.

Dr. Cabrera, the patriarch of a large family, lives in the town of Ica. He says: "I am a trained surgeon. These pictures show real surgical techniques, not some kind of rituals. They are not forgeries, either.

"And how can you explain the stones that show Indians using telescopes—thousands and thousands of years ago—when the first telescope is supposed to have been invented in 1608?"

One large round stone showed an aerial view of North and South America, as if it had been seen from a point high above Panama. Two unknown land masses were to the east and west of the isthmus. Are these the legendary lands of Atlantis and Mu?

Perhaps we have had more visitors to our small blue planet than we suspect.

Cave Paintings in the Baja

In May 1977 I spent two weeks on muleback in the mountains of the Mexican Baja. With photographer Vincent Eckersley, who curiously enough had attended the same college that I did, 8,000 miles away in England, and two archeologists, we trekked around eight of the major cave complexes in the rugged Sierra de San Francisco.

At night, our party of seven—two journalists, two archeologists, and three muleteers—slept under the stars, usually at altitudes over 5,000 feet, on the high tabletop mesas. By day, we journeyed up and down *cuestras* that led from canyon to canyon, often 3,000 feet deep.

We were dazzled by the colorful art of a people long dead. Gradually, we realized that the primitive red and black and orange paintings, done in ground stone with the chewed end of a yucca plant, contained an exciting mystery. They showed men from space!

Here were paintings made more than a thousand years ago that showed, in painstaking detail, deer, fish, and turtles. All were faithfully drawn. Yet they also showed men with arms upraised, in the same gesture of greeting depicted on the drawing NASA sent into space on the Mariner space probe. The Baja men were invariably painted with helmeted heads, often with antennae. And in one cave, *La Pintada*, which means the "Painted One," an object like a flying saucer has exhaust flames shooting out from its underside.

The archeologists in our group were baffled. They knew that these primitive Indians, the Cochimi, had no boats, no fishing equipment, and no technology when the Spanish invaders arrived in their area during the sixteenth century.

In searching for some explanation other than that men from space had once visited these remote mountains, they discovered an even stranger link. The paintings are near-duplicates of Australian aboriginal art, North African Tassili art, and Mayan and Aztec serpent motifs.

Curtis Schaafsma, an archeologist at the School of American Research, Santa Fe, suggested that we consider the possibility that the medicine men who painted on the walls of the caves were able to dip into "a pool of cosmic consciousness" and draw out the same psychic images that Australian and African and South American medicine men did.

The author and archeologists prepare to leave for the painted caves of the Baja Indians.

Frankly, I was astonished. The paintings were the same as the Australian and other art forms, yet the Cochimi could not have had physical contact with these people. Did they, then, have telepathic contact and shared images?

But images of what? Ancient astronauts? I did some more research. I found that the Australian medicine men still practice "dream time," a time when they can see, not just the past and present, but also the future. Perhaps this was a clue.

My anthropologist friends told me that the Indians of the American Southwest practiced "dream time" too. And the Baja Indians also had a religion, details of which were recorded by the Jesuits who came from Spain in the 1500s. The religion was called The Men Who Came From the Sky. In addition, the Australian, Aztec, and African tribes with similar drawings had similar legends—of the Wandjinas, a race of people with superhuman powers, who came from the land beyond the stars and the moon; winged serpents carried these gods.

I showed photographs of the cave paintings to experts around the world. Erich von Daniken, to his eternal credit, drove miles to the airport at Zurich to collect my urgent package of photographs. Later, he phoned me and said: "These are exactly like paintings I have seen at sixteen or more sites all around the world."

J. Manson Valentine, a former professor of zoology and the discoverer of the famed underground Mayan temple of X-Kukican, a discovery that won him election to the Explorers' Club, told me excitedly: "These Baja paintings show incredible correlations to paintings I have studied all over the world." Valentine told me of his searches in the Yucatan, in the mountains and plains of South America, in the Appalachian Mountains of the United States, and in France and North Africa. So many of the cave paintings show the same styles, the same subjects!

Dr. Valentine put it succinctly: "I do not believe it was an accident that the paintings of the Baja, of the Sahara, of Australia, and of peoples all over the world show similar beings, with antennae-like headdresses. The message on the rock is clear, even in the symbolic language of the medicine men. It is saying: 'We are recording the most powerful magic we have ever seen'—the magic of supermen from space."

All I know is that those long days with the mule train in 95-degree heat, when the contents of our water bottles barely kept the dust from our throats, those days when Vincent and I joked achingly about cold beer, were all worthwhile. The evidence of visitors from space was so startling that even the cactus spines hurt a little less, thinking of it....

The only way was muleback—and this photo shows the terrain the expedition covered.

The antennaelike headdresses of these cave figures have baffled experts. Are they a race memory of visitors from the stars?

Detail of cave painting from the Baja Peninsula shows mysterious manlike figure with outstretched arms and unexplained antennae headdress.

Photograph courtesy of the National ENQUIRER.

"Horn-hat" figures are painted high on this cave wall in the Baja. One of the half-red, half-black figures has arms upraised in evident greeting.

The author takes a closer look at a cave
drawing at Soledad, Baja, Mexico.

Detail of flying saucer-like object with "flames" coming from underside, from the cave wall at Soledad.

Erich von Daniken examines photographs of the Baja cave paintings at his home in Zurich, Switzerland.

Archeologist Curtis Schaafsma of Taos, New Mexico, examines a three-thou-sand-year-old Indian arrowhead. It was found in the Baja desert, close to the caves where the mysterious paintings were discovered.

These Australian cave paintings were discovered near Cape York, southern Australia. They show figures uncannily like those drawn by the Baja Indian artists. Note the upraised arms and antenna-like headdresses.

The Chain of Life

Farther north, at a cave less than 200 miles from Los Angeles, another intriguing wall painting has set experts to scratching their heads.

At first glance, this painting looks like a meaningless, colored scrawl—a jumble of zigzag lines, triangles, and rectangles. But a Swiss biologist was so intrigued by it that he redrew it as an engineering drawing, and interpreted the results. He said: "Fantastic as it might sound, I believe this shows a rough sketch of a chain-of-life reaction. It is exactly the sort of thing a geneticist might sketch. Here is a battery; here is a container for an electrostatic field; here is a zigzag to show the current; here are the triangles that depict the DNA molecular structure; here is a primitive life form, a lizard."

These things were only brought to the public's attention in 1956. Perhaps someone drew them on the wall before that? Hardly. A photograph taken by a rancher in the 1880s shows the same painting, with slightly more detail.

I asked the psychic Frederik Davies to meditate on the painting, to see if he had any constructive thoughts, because clearly this was going to be a riddle with no sure answer. His answer, if it cannot be called evidence, at least could be deemed a theory.

He opened: "It seems to me that someone, not human, was killing time in this area. Could he have been an alien, waiting to rendezvous with someone or something? Perhaps while he was waiting, he sketched an experiment, as if he was working out a mechanical means of carrying out his thoughts—a way to develop life from a test tube. And he threw the sketch away."

Later, according to Davies' theory, after the powerful gods from the sky had left, some awed Indians might have retrieved the sketch and drawn it themselves on their lonely desert cave wall, as a magic symbol.

Fanciful? Perhaps. Still, stranger things have happened.

Radio Signals from a Star

One of the strangest things in our skies today could be the result of a space probe sent out by an advanced alien civilization 13,000 years ago, when their home star was overheating their planet.

A talented young Scottish astronomer, Duncan Lunan, allowed himself the luxury of some unorthodox thinking, to the consternation of

A petroglyph (stone carving) discovered on a rock near Agadir, North Africa, in 1956. Again we see the upraised arms of the figure.

The search for life in space. Project Cyclops, our listening post to the universe,
is still only a plan. This artist's impression shows one view of the array of
radio telescopes, each as big as a football
field.

This is how the full Cyclops array will look. Between 1,000 and 2,500 radio telescopes will be used. In this view, the area covered by the radio "ear" is some eleven miles across.

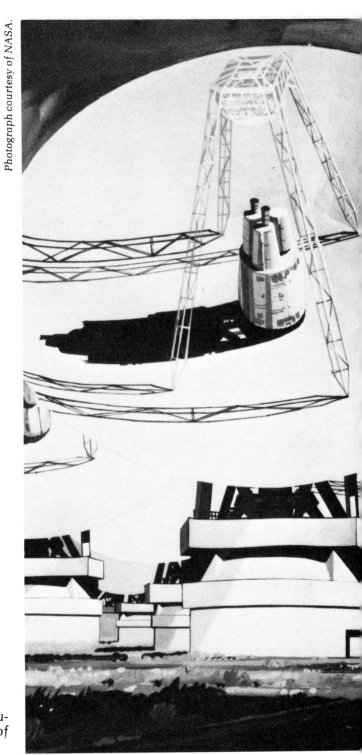

Photograph courtesy of NASA.

Detail of the Cyclops radio telescopes superimposed on an artist's rendering of the information processing center.

his more staid collegues. He took a series of mysterious radio echoes, charted in the 1920s and unexplained until today, and interpreted them as a radio "code" containing a message. In a journal, he showed how a sequence of erratic echoes, sent out as a test for what was to be Radio Hilversum in Norway, returned at intervals of up to thirty-two seconds instead of the fraction of a second response there should have been. Lunan showed how those echoes could be plotted to give a star map of the constellation Bootes. Still more echoes in the sequence filled in other stars in the same region.

Lunan speculated that the echoes were from an alien space probe sent thousands of years ago to search for intelligent life. When it eventually received radio signals, in 1928, its systems were activated. It sent its message—a star map of its home constellation—and is still patiently waiting for a reply. If the reply had been sent Lunan wondered, what other systems might have proved ready for use?

Just as the Mariner space probe to Mars and beyond carries a metal plaque showing the hydrogen atom, a sketch of our solar system, and other information available to any civilization intelligent enough to interpret it, so the alien probe sent a radio-pulsed message to us. According to Lunan, the message is: "Our home is the double star Epsilon Bootes. We live on the sixth planet of seven from the main star. Our probe is in the orbit of your moon."

But there is one catch. The star map that the probe broadcast is now 13,000 years old. Lunan knows this because Arcturus, a major landmark in the map, is misplaced in a modern galaxy, but is just where it was all those centuries ago. Perhaps that earlier civilization, desperately searching for a new home, were successful in finding one—or perhaps they perished as their star roasted their native planet.

UFO Terror

Under hypnosis, the Kentucky grandmother relived her horrifying ordeal, a nightmare of abduction by beings so terrifying that her memory refused to allow her to recall them even in the soothing calm of a hypnotherapy session.

"Help me, Lord, please," she gasped. Then, sobbing, she whispered, "It's so dark....I'm scared. Get that off my face! Please, get it off, I don't want to go to sleep." A moment later, in the quiet of the hypnotist's office, the slender woman cried out, "Please let me go home!" Then, sobbing heavily, "I want to go home. Won't somebody say something?....Don't, please don't. Don't touch me, don't. What do you *want*? Please don't touch me....Ohhh."

Moments later, after pleading to be let go, and protesting that the

Elaine Thomas, Mona Stafford, and Louise Smith are the three Kentucky women who were abducted by a UFO. Here they sit in the car in which they were riding when their ordeal began.

beings were holding her arm, in a heartbroken voice, she relived her terror: "Please, I can't do no more. I want to go home. I can't go home."

The tape recorder whirred gently as Mrs. Louise Smith turned uncomfortably. Her mind, hypnotized to help her recall the events of a January night in 1976, disgorged consciousness-buried details of the eighty terrifying minutes that are missing from her own and her two friends' lives. All three women were abducted on a lonely Kentucky road and medically examined by the unearthly, cruel crew of a UFO.

The night began normally enough. Forty-four-year-old Mrs. Smith, her friend Elaine Thomas, forty-eight, and another woman, Mona Stafford, thirty-five, were returning by car to their homes near Liberty, Kentucky, after a late supper. Suddenly a large, disk-shaped object swooped down in front of them. It was as big as a football field, gray, with a glowing white dome. Around its middle was a row of red lights. Underneath were three or four red and yellow lights. The UFO stopped in front of them, then circled behind them. The car in which they were riding surged forward at 85 miles an hour, then was dragged backward by some strong force.

Their next conscious memory was of streetlights in Hustonville, eight miles from the point where they had seen the UFO at 11:30 P.M. And by this time it was 1:25 A.M.

Physical examination showed they all three women had strange red marks on their necks, "like a fresh burn that had not blistered," three inches long and an inch wide. The women reported that water "burned and burned" their faces. They were very thirsty, weak, and felt "drained of life." Six months later, after the women were put under hypnosis to relive their experience, the same red marks reappeared on them.

The raw terror that hypnosis brought to light was not faked, either. Mrs. Smith, in a weak voice, told the beings: "I want to see you, let me see you. Let me look at your eyes, I can't hurt you." And in the doctor's office, she opened her eyes, looked around for an instant, then collapsed in terror, sobbing, "No. I don't want to see no more. Please, I want to go home, please let me go home." Then, after a moment of silence, she whispered, "I want to die."

The other women showed similar reactions. Elaine Thomas complained in fear of the weight on her chest and sobbed that something was pressing down on her throat because it didn't want her to talk. She coughed and choked, time and again. "I'm afraid they'll hear me because

Mona Stafford readily underwent a polygraph test designed to check the truthfulness of her statements concerning her UFO abduction.

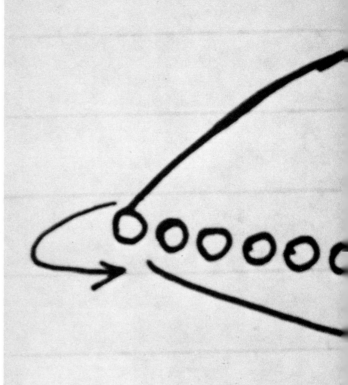

This is Mona Stafford's own felt pen sketch of the strange craft that abducted her and her companions and subjected them to medical-type tests.

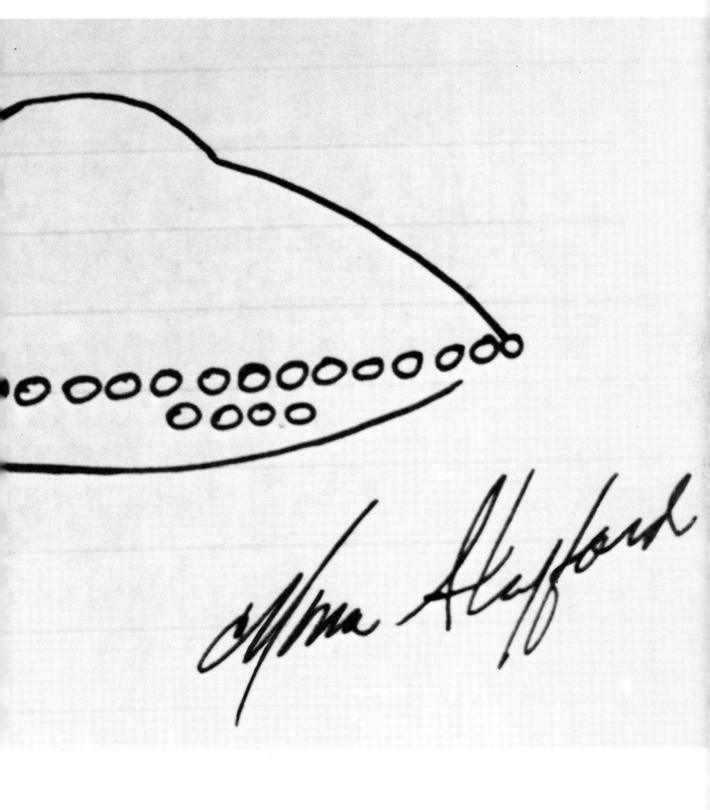

they choked me. They won't let me talk."

The hypnotist, Leo R. Sprinkle, an associate professor at the University of Wyoming, asked her if They knew that she was in pain. "I knew that they knew. But they didn't care," she sobbed.

She recalled seeing a pair of eyes above her. "These two eyes floated toward me. They came real close. One was a beautiful blue and the other was dark, in the shadows. I couldn't tell the color. He looked so cruel. He just looked down at me. I tried to grasp the expression in that eye. I can't tell what he was meaning, but he meant something...."

Mona Stafford also saw an eye under hypnosis. "It's kind of like a crystal," she explained. "It just comes back and forth to me. It just bursts into light or something after a while, like there's something in it. The eye is like a door or something."

Mona cried aloud during her hypnosis sessions, too, remembering tortures that the aliens made her undergo. She felt her stomach "blowing up," her neck being held fast. Her hand was numb, then swollen, and she screamed aloud as the beings seemed to force her feet backward. "My feet are being bent backward. I can't take no more," she moaned.

Dr. Sprinkle, who noted that it is extremely difficult for a subject under hypnosis to lie, said he "firmly believed" the women were describing real experiences. "The chance they have lied is beyond all reasonable possibility," said the doctor.

But for these UFO victims, their trauma may not have ended yet. For there are reports of a new and mysterious phenomenon: the men in black.

The Men in Black

In a bright suburban home in San Antonio, the doorbell rang. The young, blonde housewife opened it. Outside, hunched up in black overcoats, gray-faced despite the bright Texas sunshine, two small, spindly-looking men stood. The housewife shivered. She remembered the sighting, two weeks earlier, that her husband had made of a pebble-shaped UFO.

"What is your name?" asked one of the visitors, who seemed to be standing with some difficulty.

Artist Bob Steven's imagination may not be all that bizarre. The "little green men from Mars" were superimposed on a view of the Martian surface in the Chryse area that was taken just before sunset; hence the long shadows.

When the housewife didn't reply, he repeated the question. Nervously, she murmured that they must be at the wrong house.

"Are you Mrs. Schorah?" the other man asked.

After she admitted that this was her name, they asked to come inside to discuss "a matter of importance." She refused, asking them to call later when her husband was home.

Then one, clearly the leader of the two, asked if her husband had seen anything in the sky recently. His voice was harsh and difficult to understand.

Mrs. Schorah felt a jolt of fright again, but she nodded, dumbly.

"You must warn your husband not to draw any hasty conclusions from what he saw," the leader warned. With that, the pair turned and walked slowly away down the street.

Mrs. Schorah—the name is fictitious—kept the incident to herself until a few nights later, when she and her husband, Mike, were watching television. The set began to flicker on and off and to emit an odd, humming sound. All the lights in the house began to go off and on, too.

Sobbing, and somehow connecting the incidents, the young wife told her husband about the visitors. The husband angrily sent for an electrician, who could find nothing wrong with the house wiring.

A month later, another "man in black" came to the house. This time, Mike was at home. Mrs. Schorah saw the man, who was wearing a black raincoat, painfully get out of a parked Nova and walk up to her husband. The stranger was not one of the original pair.

"The guy looked sick and weak to me," recalls Mike. "He leaned over as I was doing some repair work on my driveway and asked what I was doing. I mumbled something about home repairs. Then he reached out and touched me, without even letting his hand emerge from his sleeve. He said, simply, 'Be careful.' Then he walked off, got into his car, and drove away."

Days later, Mike swears he saw the same man watching him on a street corner in San Antonio. After this, odd things began to happen to Mike. His digital watch started to run backward, or to blink on and off for no apparent reason. He purchased a new watch and it did the same. Electrical equipment in the house began to switch itself on and off. The television set came on in the middle of the night, even though it was unplugged.

These odd phenomena continued to happen for four years. Abruptly, in 1974, they all ceased. Life is now back to normal for the Schorahs. They hope....

Interestingly, although the U.S. Air Force officially ended its investigation of UFOs in 1969, the Surgeon General at the Institute for Aerospace Medicine, located near Mike's home, at Randolph Air Force Base, Texas, monitors the physical, mental, and emotional state of people who have seen flying saucers even after they have been discharged. Some of the phenomena that plagued Mike are not unknown elsewhere. Louise Smith, one of the three abducted Kentucky women, noticed that her watch "acted funny." The minute hand went round almost as fast as the second hand after she returned home that fateful evening.

"Men in black" are frequently reported by the public. Often they seem to be simply observing their human "targets" after UFO sightings. Descriptions by witnesses are remarkably similar, although few accounts of these men appear in any but occult or UFO magazines, and then only rarely. Time after time, witnesses talk of strange men, often wearing heavy overcoats (and incongruously, sunglasses). Often they are small, thin men, stooped over. Some observers feel that they are hunched up because of the strain of coping with the "heavy" gravity forces on Earth.

Lieutenant Colonel James R. Doherty, USAF retired, had a close encounter with a UFO on June 21, 1951. He was cruising at 21,000 feet over the Mediterranean in his F-84G Thunderjet. He checked the tail of his plane and noted a plate-shaped object about twenty feet in diameter behind him. It gave off an intense light, the color of "molten steel."

For twenty minutes the two flying machines were pitted in aerial maneuvers as the pilot attempted to evade his adversary. Abruptly, the UFO veered away. The pilot landed and filed a report, then forgot about it. But not for long.

"A few days after my encounter," he recalls, "a skinny young lieutenant came to talk to me. He was in an Air Force raincoat, emaciated. His thin face was twisted up as if he was in pain. He told me he was from the Air Force Office of Special Investigations. His voice was odd, heavily accented. He warned me to forget about my encounter with the UFO."

Shortly afterward, the pilot was visiting the Special Investigations office on another matter and asked to see this same lieutenant. "I described him—but no one of that description had ever worked there."

For years after that, Doherty was haunted by uncanny events related to that sighting. His copy of the report mysteriously vanished from his home; letters to other officers describing the incident never arrived. For months, every photograph he took was fogged in a way that technicians could not explain. Electrical appliances in his home acted oddly.

And Doherty has had a recurrent nightmare. In it he sees a man who very closely resembles the skinny OSI officer.

THE AMAZING POWER
OF MINDPOWER

Telepathy, the ability to understand the unspoken thoughts of another person, is the best-known psychic phenomenon. Instances of telepathy, often placed under the all-embracing term ESP, an acronym for extrasensory perception, are fairly common: twins experience each other's pain or terror, or a husband and wife voice the same thought at the same moment. But the vast majority of us think of ESP in terms of the psychic who predicts the future—usually with a disappointingly low rate of success.

Clarisa Bernhardt

One of the more impressive psychics is Clarisa Bernhardt, who lives in Los Gatos, California. Clarisa, blonde, pigtailed, and irrepressibly bubbly, is married to an actor, Russ Bernhardt. Clarisa came to national prominence in 1974 when she predicted, on a local radio station in Los Gatos, that the "central coast area will experience a quake at three P.M. on Thursday, November 28. It will be quite a jolt, but there will be no injuries and property damage will be minor. There is no cause for alarm." The tremors struck on the date she predicted, disrupting the police radio system in San Benito and causing minor damage across a widespread area. And, as she predicted, no one was hurt. The time of the quake was 3:01 P.M.—Clarisa was one minute off in her prediction.

Clarisa made another pinpoint-accurate prediction to me personally. She forecast two earthquakes during 1975. One, she said, would happen in the Northern Hemisphere on November 29, the other in the Southern Hemisphere on May 25. She repeated her predictions in print, months before the events. To Australian journalist Jeff Kirkwood, she even specified that the Northern Hemisphere quake would hit the Hawaiian Islands.

Again, Clarisa was right, or almost right. Hawaii was rocked by its worst earthquake in a century on the exact date she predicted. On her second prediction she had the wrong geographic location, but she did name the exact date in the year when the world's worst earthquake hit.

David Stewart, director of the prestigious MacCarthy Geophysics Laboratory, at the University of North Carolina, told me: "I am an earthquake seismologist and I am tremendously impressed by Mrs. Bernhardt's predictions. She picked the two days when the two worst earthquakes hit—a 7.6 Richter scale quake in the Azores, and one measuring 7.2 in Hawaii. Her prediction defied huge odds."

How does she do it? I asked Clarisa this question when I met her and here is her answer:

"I sense a change in the atmosphere when an earthquake is imminent. There are certain radiations the earth gives off, and they seem to come to me, so that I know something is wrong. For instance, I sense that there will be a volcanic eruption in Oregon. The volcano is dormant now, but by March 1978 it will let itself be known—although nobody will be injured." (The United States Geological Service reports there are no known dormant volcanoes in Oregon, only extinct ones.)

Where, I asked Clarisa, did she obtain specifics such as dates and times for a random event like an earthquake?

"I have been psychic since I was a child," she explained in a matter-of-fact manner. "I see and hear psychically, although I cannot explain just how. It's not a spooky thing. I simply get impressions, just as if I am looking at a movie screen.

"To get those dates [on the 1975 earthquakes], for example, I closed my eyes. I got an impression, in black and white, of a date. It was just like the page of a calendar. Unmistakably, it said November 29. It was so definite, so positive, that I knew I was right."

Nowadays, whenever Clarisa Bernhardt gets an impression, she logs it with the United States Geological Survey at Boulder, Colorado. There, a team of scientists is attempting to decide *what* she is receiving and, if possible, to find out *how* she receives it.

Long-Distance Telepathy

Psychics do not always predict doom and disaster. One of my favorite psychics, Swedish-born Olof Jonsson, is a middle-aged engineer

California psychic Clarisa Bernhardt is called the "Earthquake Lady" for her uncanny ability to predict accurately the time and place of earthquakes.

who now lives in Chicago. Olof has an impressive history of psychic research. He has been tested and retested by all kinds of researchers and endures all their procedures with astonishing good nature.

Olof's finest moment came when he and astronaut Edgar Mitchell collaborated in a test of telepathy during Mitchell's lunar flight on Apollo 14. Astronaut Mitchell attempted to "send" number and symbol images to the earthbound psychic. The experiment was a statistical success, with results of better than 3,000 to 1 probability.

This test of telepathy was in some respects a repeat of the Arctic experiments of 1937. At that time, Arkansas psychic Harold Sherman successfully "saw" a fire and recorded other thoughts, feelings, and impressions of a cooperating explorer in the frozen north.

Again, there was no possibility of using normal methods of communication. Explorer and psychic kept detailed, dated notes, which were compared months after the events. Those notes showed the unbelievable. At the very time that the psychic had seen and recorded images of fire, the worst disaster of the expedition had happened: fire had destroyed one of their huts, with all its stored equipment.

The explorer was Sir Hubert Wilkins, who was at the time searching for a lost Soviet airplane crew. Wilkins spent five and a half months in the polar regions and kept a meticulous log. Psychic Harold Sherman, on his part, "recorded some hundreds of impressions, and it was found, on checking against Wilkins' diary, that some 70 percent of them were remarkably accurate—scored as genuine hits."

Sherman is a soft-spoken, white-haired, grandfatherly figure. He told me how he first encountered the power of his psychic functioning: "It took place in 1915, when I was seventeen years old. I was in my room on the second floor of our family home in Traverse City, Michigan, at my typewriter. It was late afternoon and the sun was setting. I got up to turn on the light, which was suspended from the center of the ceiling. As I reached for the switch above the bulb, a voice in my inner ear—not any voice that I heard externally—said, 'Don't turn on the light.'

"I had never before received such an eerie impression. I couldn't go against it. I returned to my typewriter and typed for about another ten minutes, but it was getting so dark I had to do something. I fixed my attention on the light again, but before I could touch the switch, I was warned

Harold Sherman is the Arkansas psychic who conducted long-distance ESP tests with an Arctic explorer in the 1930s. He has also had spectacular success in mental fly-pasts of the planets of our solar system.

*Chicago psychic Olaf Joinsson conducted
ESP tests with astronaut Edgar Mitchell.*

Apollo 14's lunar module pilot, Captain Edgar Mitchell, at Kennedy Space Center in Florida. Mitchell's moon flight gave him a deep awareness of psychic functioning.

Captain Mitchell on the moon's surface. Here he is using a pull cart as a mobile workbench to adjust a portable magnetometer designed to measure the moon's magnetic field.

more emphatically than before: 'Don't turn on the light.'

"At that moment someone ran up on the porch and banged on the door. I went downstairs, without turning on the light, to see an electric light lineman, whose first, urgent words were, 'Don't turn on the light! There's a high-voltage wire down across your line outside.'

"I realized that, in ways I didn't understand, I had somehow tuned into the mind of the lineman. He told me he had reported on a trouble call about ten minutes before and had found not only our line, but also those of two neighbors, in contact with the fallen high-voltage wire. His one thought was to warn the residents as quickly as possible.

"I doubt if anything serious would have happened to me," Sherman continued, as he sat stroking a ginger and white cat, "but I was deeply impressed by the fact that I had picked up the one dominant, emotionalized thought in that lineman's mind."

After that experience, the fledgling psychic tried experiments with friends. In one, he practiced waking a friend at a given hour without telling the friend of his plan. "I practiced saying, 'Homer, you are going to wake up and think of me when the clock strikes two tonight.' And I did it over and over, for about ten minutes, until a strange feeling came over me, as if some energy had left me and gone to him. Next morning, Homer rang me up asking me if I'd tried to wake him. When I said I had, he told me: 'That's it. I woke up suddenly as the town clock was striking two, with the feeling you were in the room with me. You scared the hell out of me."

Sherman has spent a lifetime in psychic research and founded an organization called ESP Research Center in Mountain View, Arkansas. The group's last convention—an annual event in St. Louis—attracted some 2,000 participants.

Jeane Dixon

Jeane Dixon is probably America's best-known psychic. She is something of an enigma because she keeps her private life, and much of her public life, away from public scrutiny. Jeane Dixon has been remarkably accurate in some of her predictions; in others, she has been dramatically wrong. Yet she does have an uncanny ability to make specific predictions. She forecast the deaths of both John and Robert Kennedy. She predicted the name of the future president of Mexico five years before the event. She predicted President Carter's election eight months ahead

Two of America's top psychics, Fredrick Davies and Jeane Dixon, sit in the courtyard of Mrs. Dixon's home in Washington, D.C. The author is standing behind them.

Photograph courtesy of the National ENQUIRER.

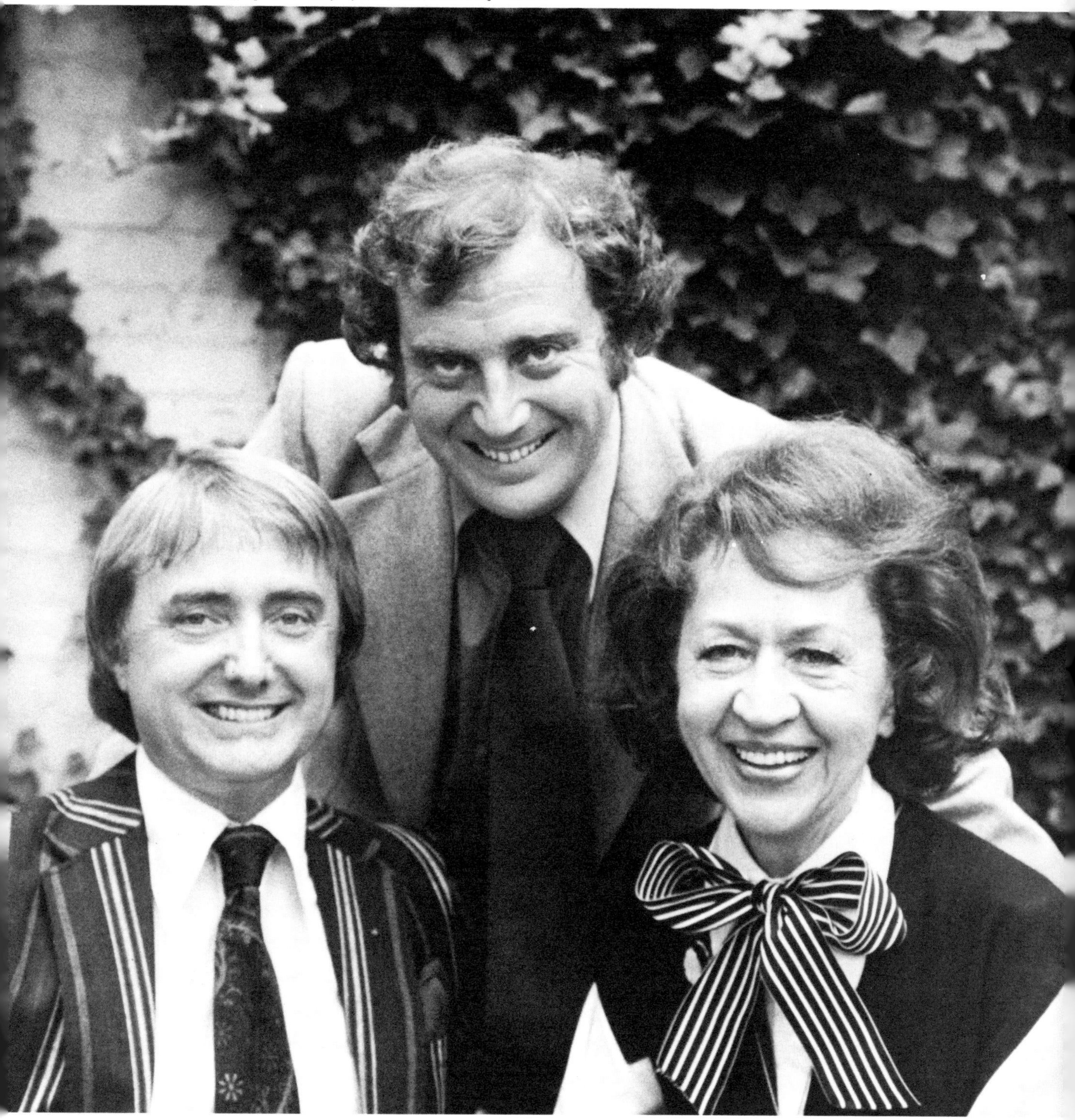

of time, when he was only one of a handful of Democratic contenders, and not an important one at that.

But, for all that, Jeane's ability to predict the future may not be her greatest gift. She uses ESP differently. In face-to-face contact, she can sense the "vibrations" of a new acquaintance. She constantly astonishes people with her accurate readings of their past and future. This seems to be a valid form of "extra knowing," an extra sense. No one knows how she does it. Her own explanation is that "God programs all our lives, and I am able to read into those programs, by feeling a person's fingertips."

The Prophecies of Nostradamus

Dramatic evidence of ESP can be found throughout history. One of the best-documented seers is Nostradamus, the medieval French prophet who has an eerie record of successful predictions. Perhaps more interesting is the fact that some of the prophecies of Nostradamus are still coming true.

Nostradamus wrote in baffling quatrains—four-line verses—but they were clear enough and detailed enough for people to see that he had forecast, two hundred years before the event, the arrest of the French king Louis XVI and the name of the man who betrayed him. Nostradamus also named Napoleon, in an anagram, and told of his rise to power; named General Franco; and forecast a World War II summit meeting.

Equally incredibly, the bearded seer also forecast the dates of the Great Fire of London, the French Revolution, and a church conference that persecuted astrologers. His forecasts for the future include a world war in 1999, "a great king of terror who will descend from the skies," and an Arab conqueror who will wage a bloody war that will last twenty-seven years.

Stewart Robb, who teaches at a California college, has studied the thousand prophecies of Nostradamus carefully. Says Robb: Allowing for the fact that Nostradamus was French and that the future of France and its kings was of prime importance to him, his prophecies in general are uncannily accurate. He talked of the government of America when America was a howling wilderness; he spoke of the 'Empire of England' in the 1500s, when England was just another nation. He was very exact in his choice of words. For example, he said that 'people will travel safely through the sky, land, sea and wave.' He specified 'sea and wave.' Ships pass through the wave, submarines through the sea."

Yet Nostradamus died in 1566, and it was fifty years later that the first of his prophecies came true. ESP? In this case, did prophecy somehow tune into future events, just as telepathy tunes into another's thoughts in the present?

A pen-and-ink drawing by Bruce Benjamin of Nostradamus, the medieval seer whose poetic prophecies have been coming true for hundreds of years.

Teaching ESP

It would appear obvious, then, that ESP is not restricted simply to reading another person's thoughts. It is a blanket term for any experience or contact with another event or state—or person or object—without the use of the normal human senses. Recently, attention has focused on whether or not ESP can be learned.

Charles Tart, a gentle, slightly rumpled-looking professor at the University of California, has worked with volunteer students, to "teach" them ESP. Where does all this leave us? If ESP can be taught in a laboratory, can be carried over thousands of miles, can be something a psychic picks up from another person's fingertips, or can be used to predict events fifty years in the future, what exactly is it? Professor Tart points out that his students were selected for their evident psychic ability, that the ESP test was only a statistical test, and that it was designed to provide a relatively steady flow of ESP for laboratory testing. His techniques, among them one of instantly telling his students if their mechanical guessing-game routine was successful or not, were successful in helping the students beat odds of a million billion billions to one—odds so great that, expressed in figures, the number would have 25 zeroes behind it.

Charles Tart says that he has simply helped people to understand their own ESP and how it works. This, in turn, has helped them develop their own abilities. In truth, Tart's ESP teaching machine —prosaically called a ten-choice trainer—doesn't seem too dramatic. But it may lead to a better understanding of how the human mind works. At the least, it seems to make ESP repeatable, under test conditions in the scientists' laboratories.

A New Channel of Communication

Two American physicists think ESP is an as yet undiscovered channel of communication. Harold Puthoff and Russell Targ work at the world-famous Stanford Research Institute. Both scientists are relatively young men—Puthoff is thirty-nine and Targ is forty-three—and both are extremely talented researchers.

The two men investigated psychic Uri Geller. Although they were personally convinced that Geller had some distinct psychic ability, they were unable to find any proof of it under stringent scientific conditions, or even to present anything that would stand as "scientific" evi-

Dr. Harold Puthoff, senior research engineer at the Stanford Research Institute in California.

dence. Puthoff and Targ are ethical scientists and are bound by the disciplines of science to report their findings professionally. They were sufficiently interested, however, to investigate other psychic phenomena.

They hit upon a series of tests they called "remote viewing." It was, in fact, a perfect example of ESP at work. The way they achieved the breakthrough has the element of the comic about it that characterizes much psychic research. Fortunately, Puthoff and Targ are confident enough about their abilities to tell this story against themselves.

"I was casually interested in popular reports of ESP research, but did not become professionally involved until 1972," comments Hal Puthoff, a dark-haired, engagingly frank person. "Then, after a series of events, I invited Ingo Swann, a New York artist, to Stanford for a week of experiments on biological effects.

"Ingo became part of my life for the next year. I found him good-humored, thoughtful, and articulate. I conducted some tests with him, with good results, and eventually asked him to work with us oever an extended period of time.

"I recall one test of that early series particularly. Two visitors representing a potential sponsor put Ingo through a series of ten experiments in which he had to say what they had hidden in a box. I was amazed when, in one of the tests, Ingo said, 'I see something small, brown, and irregular, sort of like a leaf or something that resembles it—except that it seems very much alive; it's even moving.' The target turned out to be a small live moth, which did indeed look like a leaf!"

After that first series of experiments, Swann began a longer series of ESP tests. Russell Targ, who had recently joined Puthoff, takes up the story: "Ingo began to fret somewhat at our boring, statistically based tests and began to harass us to do some other, more interesting experiments. He suggested that we replicate some experiments he had done at the American Society for Psychical Research, during which he had described in detail things at some faraway location. I remember the awkward silence when he made his suggestion. We had had enough difficulty with our own, carefully conceived experiments, and now here he was, proposing something that sounded infinitely more difficult. We promised to think about it—and promptly didn't. But Ingo then volunteered to do the experiments during our coffee breaks. How could we argue?"

Still, the two academics must have shuffled their feet at Ingo's

New York artist Ingo Swann stands in front of one of his paintings. Among Swann's abilities is the gift of being able to describe a terrain exactly from any given set of map coordinates.

unscientific approach. Today, they have the grace to acknowledge the irony of it all. For those coffee-break "games" of ESP brought about what is now recognized as the key breakthrough in parapsychology research—the repeatable experiment that scientists have been striving for since the days of the Victorian parapsychologists.

Ingo, a talented artist whose ability to visualize images must have some bearing on his psychic performance, sat down with a list of ten sets of map coordinates, which Puthoff and Targ had taken from a world map in another room. In a twenty-minute test, Ingo rattled off brief responses to each set of coordinates and scored 70 percent right. (A random guesser would score perhaps fifteen percent correct.)

"He'd say something like 'land, jungles, peninsular mountains' in response to our 'fifteen degrees north, one hundred twenty degrees east,'" recalls Targ. "We thought it wasn't bad, but we also considered the possibility that he was well informed on the geographical features of the earth and their approximate location by latitude and longitude."

The two physicists tried another series. This time they were trickier; they chose small bodies of water in large land masses, or small islands in the middle of oceans. Yet the psychic never faltered. Even when his responses were a bit ambiguous here or a bit vague there, they were sufficiently accurate to make the Stanford researchers wonder what they had uncovered.

In all, Ingo made ten series of ten sets of descriptions—one hundred individual descriptions—and scored on the order of 70 percent throughout. In the last series, for example, he made seven hits in ten tries, had two descriptions judged neutral, and made one clear miss. His correct answers were sometimes spectacular. For example, in "two degrees south, thirty-four degrees east" (the eastern shore of Lake Victoria, Africa), Ingo described a sense of speeding over water and landing on land, with a lake to the west and high elevation.

"The amazing thing to us," says Targ, "was that we had chosen these coordinates to correspond to the middle of Lake Victoria—and Ingo insisted that they triggered a picture of land to the right of a large lake. So we checked with a detailed map of the area—and found that he was right."

Ingo Swann, the armchair viewer, performed even more stunningly in another test, when the vital coordinates were supplied by

Stanford Research Institute's Laser Physicist Russel Targ stands in New York City outside Grant's Tomb, the psychic viewing "target" successfully observed from thousands of miles away.

Grant's Tomb, New York City.

someone whom Targ and Puthoff describe as a "government scientist."

Recalls Puthoff: "We received the coordinates 'forty-nine degrees twenty minutes south, seventy degrees fourteen minutes east', by telephone from the scientist. He was challenging our work. No maps were permitted and Swann was asked to reply immediately. He said: 'My initial response is that it's an island, maybe a mountain sticking up through cloud cover. Terrain seems rocky, must be some sort of small plants growing there. Cloud bank to the west. Very cold. I see some buildings rather mathematically laid out. One of them is orange. There is something like a radar antennae, a round disk.'"

"Swann drew a map and continued: 'Two white cylindrical tanks, quite large. To the northwest, a small airstrip. Wind is blowing. Must be two or three trucks in front of a building. Behind, is that an outhouse? There's not much there.'"

Puthoff had by now consulted his transcript of the tape-recorded experiment, to repeat verbatim all that Ingo had described about the coastline of the island, drawing segments as he mentally "flew over" it. He had described rocks sticking up out of the ocean, hills in the west, flatlands and an airstrip in the north. He had supplied other details, sketching them onto a map and specifying just where everything was.

Incredibly, the artist-psychic's drawings and descriptions fitted almost exactly the target island: a remote spot in the southern Indian Ocean. Called Kerguelen, the island is administered as part of the French southern and Antarctic lands and serves as a French base for upper-atmosphere meteorological studies. Swann had pinpointed the one population center of the island, in the northeast sector, and had drawn it in on his map. He had found the one mountain, in the west, and had sketched a coastline remarkably like the real one.

I was impressed by what the two physicists had told me. Yet, I thought perhaps Swann could have obtained all that information from a map. I tracked down an expert and phoned him at his office in Paris.

Jean Rivolier's title is Chief of Medicine and Research, Laboratories for the French Antarctic. He has spent considerable time on the lonely, rocky outpost of his country's former empire. He confirmed the general descriptions made by the psychic and then related the following details: "Yes, there are some white cylinders with fuel oil in them, and there is a radio antenna. There isn't an orange building, but there is an orange-colored wall that was put up to protect the meteorological equipment from the wind. The buildings *are* arranged geometrically. There is one settlement on the island; other than that, there are just a few mountain refuge huts. There is no airstrip, but to the northwest of the huts, as your psychic said, there is a flattened area that, from the air, could easily be mistaken for an airstrip. These descriptions are very good indeed. I find it hard to believe that someone who has not been to the island could make them."

When I spoke to Ingo Swann, he said: "Of course I have never been to the island—and I haven't read about it or seen any material about it either. I was simply able to flipflop back and forth between my mind—traveling half the world away to an unknown location—and my body, sitting comfortably on that imitation-leather sofa at Stanford."

He explained his strange accomplishments this way: "It meant I could see what was, say, in Siberia, then talk about it and describe it to Dr. Puthoff. Then I'd flip back for another look, come back and describe what I saw, and so on. I sometimes went high in the sky for an overall view; sometimes I would focus in very closely to look at specifics.

"As I used the techniques, after about sixty sets of coordinates I would become aware of a sensation of speeding over the land I was looking at. I'd hear the wind, feel the cold, see grass waving in the wind. I remember that when I looked at Kerguelen, I saw a mountain sticking up out of clouds, went down to look at it, and found it was covered in bird lime!"

Is Ingo Swann the only person in the world with this incredible ability? According to Drs. Targ and Puthoff, every one of us has it. And they have scientific facts to support their belief. For, after the successful series of tests with Swann, they began several years of testing with talented psychics, ordinary people, and downright disbelievers.

In April 1977 they presented their findings of "what could be a new channel of communication" to an international electronics convention in New York. They told how dozens of tests yielded high-quality results. Amazingly good responses from so-called psychically untalented people are not rare. And they reported that even copper and steel shielding cannot stop these mental-energy transmissions.

Targ and Puthoff tell the full story of their work in their book *Mind Reach* (1977), but here are some highlights of it. Their tests are simple enough. One or two experimenters go to a randomly chosen site and at a prearranged time simply make sure they are aware of their surroundings. Back in the laboratory, the test subject records his impressions of what the experimenters are seeing, much as Ingo Swann recorded his impressions of what was at the coordinate's target.

Another scientist checks for fair play. Later, a panel of independent judges attempts to match what the subject "saw" with the scientific target pool of ten or twenty sites. Invariably the correlations are very high, often 80 to 90 percent accurate.

Sometimes the test subject "sees" the target from above and not from the viewpoint of the testers. Sometimes the test subject "sees" the target minutes before the testers get there. Once, in a strictly controlled test, a subject even saw an underground target. At times a subject has named the exact place the testers went.

Other scientists—John Bisaha of Mundelein College, Chicago, is one—have repeated similar experiments with equal success. Researchers from other countries are interested, too. The Russians are doing similar work. John Hasted, one of the British team that helped develop radar during World War II, now heads the Department of Experimental Physics at Birkbeck College, London. While Targ and Puthoff deny that government agencies are funding their work, Hasted is outspoken.

"One ever knows for certain what work is going on in secret," Hasted told me. "I suspect that all governments are keenly interested. I have heard extensive rumors about a Soviet psychical research laboratory in the Crimea. There seems to be no reason at all why one day a spy couldn't psychically overview a target, and perhaps transfer his thoughts onto photographic film. I believe that the Soviets and other governments are investigating possibilities like this. We already know that some psychics can look at targets thousands of miles away—completely undetected."

Ingo Swann, too, has heard these rumors. "I believe that the Russians are concentrating on developing this long-distance psychic viewing, he says. "I have heard this from several different sources."

There could be other, better uses for this incredible talent. We could use it to explore the oceans, the undersurface of the earth, or the outer reaches of space. There is almost no limit to the possibilities in the relatively unknown area of the human mind.

The Psychic Vikings

Edgar Mitchell, described by *Time* magazine as the "most cerebral of the astronauts," considers the exploration of outer space less important than the exploration of "inner space"—the mind. Coming from Mitchell, the sixth man ever to walk on the face of the moon, such a statement cannot be regarded lightly. Yet many of today's Vikings are exploring the reaches of their own minds.

Psychics Harold Sherman and Ingo Swann became the world's farthest-traveled "psychic Vikings" when they set out to "view" the planet Jupiter. In the "ordinary" way this undertaking cost the United States government billions of dollars in the spaceship Pioneer 10. In psychic travel it merely meant that Harold sat comfortably in his home in the beautiful Ozark Mountains, and Ingo reported to the Stanford laboratory

for a simultaneous out-of-body experience and psychic fly-past of the giant planet. The two psychics recorded similar impressions—crystals, yellowish color, clouds, an undramatic horizon with mountain peaks nearby, winds, water, and curiously enough, difficulty of movement. The test is still unresolved, although the Pioneer spacecraft confirmed some of their impressions, but it does point up the possibilities.

Another test of long-distance viewing was reported by a young Arizona-based archeologist, Jeffrey Goodman. Goodman hit upon the idea of having a psychic pinpoint the site of an ancient human settlement. After certain preliminary tests, an Oregon psychic, Aron Abrahamsen, found a site that has created some ferment in the archeological world.

Abrahamsen went into a self-induced trance, flew out of body, and noted several sites. He reported: "There, I saw a mother, a member of a primitive Indian tribe, lying asleep with her two children. Their pack pony was tethered nearby. In seconds, tragedy struck as an ice wall collapsed on top of them."

Goodman led a team of archeologists from the University of Arizona to the site that Abrahamson had pinpointed down to an area ten yards square. Even Goodman had doubts. "The site seemed unlikely to me—I was convinced by Aron. It was a million-to-one geological formation, and all the experts I consulted before the dig said it would be impossible to find traces of humans there."

But as the diggers went into the earth, they were astonished to find rock formations exactly as the psychic had predicted. At last count, the team had found stone chopping tools 100,000 years old, some wood, fossil soil, and pollen traces. Abrahamsen has so far been 88 percent accurate in his predictions, as analyzed by computers. "It's impressive when you think that trained archeologists felt we shouldn't even have dug at the site," Goodman exulted.

It seemed incredible. I asked about the ancient Indians who are supposed to have died in that tragedy a thousand centuries ago. "We haven't found them yet," the archeologist said, "but I'm certain we will when we get to the depth Aron indicated. He's been right at every level so far."

I left him, wondering anew at our psychic abilities and how they could be developed even further. If we can explore the depths of space, forecast the future, and tune into the past, what else can we do?

The space probe Pioneer, *shown here in an artist's impression, over the famous Red Spot of Jupiter. The probe's findings confirmed with astonishing accuracy the impressions of psychics Swann and Sherman.*

Archeologist Jeffrey Goodman holds a stone axhead that is 80,000 years old. It was found deep in the sandy soil of Arizona, just where a psychic told him it would be.

Here is Dr. Goodman's excavation site near Flagstaff, Arizona. The wooden boxlike structure is the top of the hole. The boom connected to the pail is used to bring material to the surface, where it is sifted for examination.

CHAPTER 6.

PSYCHIC KNOWLEDGE OR PSYCHIC WAR?

The Strange Powers
of Nina and Felicia

Interaction with the things that surround us—with our own personal universes—is a key to understanding much of psychic functioning. Many researchers believe that we create our own surroundings, we shape the events that happen around us and are much more in control of so-called inanimate objects than we suspect.

A few people seem to have found the answer to making so-called inanimate matter react to them. Uri Geller is one. The extraordinary children, Julie Knowles and David Shepherd are two others. But the Soviets have chanced upon one of the world's most powerful psychics, Leningrad-born Nina Kulagina.

The full range of Mrs. Kulagina's abilities is a closely guarded secret, but witnesses to her psychic powers and movie film about her tell at least part of her incredible story. One of the best witnesses is Jarl Fahler, a researcher in the department of psychology at the University of Helsinki, Finland. Dr. Fahler, along with Tasmanian researcher Jurgen Keil, traveled to Leningrad for a rare meeting with the Soviet psychic. They dined with her, then began some psychokinetic tests to see if she could move objects by mindpower.

Nina succeeded in moving objects that were contained in clear plastic cases that the two researchers had brought to the meeting. She spun a compass needle, then moved the entire compass. She also moved a small wineglass that was upside down and covered by a larger wineglass. In all, she moved about thirty small objects in a half hour.

Dr. Fahler decided to try another experiment. "I had heard that Nina had been able on previous occasions to induce heat and pain effects on people's flesh, by simply touching them. I was skeptical. I am a trained psychologist, and I was confident that it would be impossible for her to suggest a psychosomatic feeling of pain in me."

The fifty-year-old psychologist rolled up his sleeve, put a thermometer between his arm and Nina's hand, and prepared to see what the psychic could do. This experiment was also filmed by a movie camera.

"After about thirty seconds," reported Dr. Fahler, "I felt heat and pain. The sensation increased in intensity until after two or three minutes it became almost unbearable. I remember thinking, with amazement, that this could not be happening. Yet it did happen."

There was no rise in the thermometer's reading, yet the burn marks on Dr. Fahler's arm are clearly visible in the movie record. The skin was red and burned, like a bad sunburn. Astonishingly, next morning the burn marks had simply vanished. They had left no blisters or aftereffects.

"I was burned by an unknown force, some mysterious energy that we know nothing about," says Dr. Fahler.

Dr. Keil, the psychologist from the University of Tasmania, who accompanied Jarl Fahler, had tested Nina once before, as part of a University of Virginia study in 1973. He watched the burn marks appear on his colleague's arm and decided to see if he could shield his own arm by putting a piece of lead partially between the psychic's hand and his skin.

"The sensation was definitely that the lead blocked whatever produced the heat sensation," he reported. "I experienced a heat sensation that seemed utterly real and unpleasant, but it did not increase beyond that level."

Today, Nina Kulagina is kept away from Western researchers. Reports reach the West that she and other top Soviet psychics are treated like royalty and are being carefully investigated for an explanation of their uncanny powers. For the Soviets, ever alert to the possibility of a military use for new developments, in this case mindpower, have mounted a massive and secret research program concerning psychic powers.

Compare Nina Kulagina's case with that of a talented American psychic. Before the Soviets went "underground" with their psychic research, Kulagina was world-famous among parapsychologists. Yet in New York, a slim, auburn-haired Brooklyn woman, Felicia Parise, was doing the same things. Nobody but a few underfunded researchers knew or cared. She developed her powers to a certain point, then gave up.

I heard about this woman, now a leukemia researcher at a New York hospital, and verified her strong psychic powers. Among her accomplishments, she could:

- cause a small bottle to slide backward and forward
- move corks, tinfoil strips, and a compass needle
- create a baffling "energy field" in a laboratory
- score 80 percent in ESP tests
- cause unexposed film in sealed packets to fog over

In laboratory tests Felicia affected a compass needle, making it deflect 15 degrees from true north. When the testers picked up the compass and placed it several feet away from Felicia, the needle swung back to true north. Returned to its original position, in Felicia's "force field," it promptly turned 15 degrees away again. It took a half hour before the mysterious effect wore off.

Yet Felicia Parise has quietly let these powers go. "I have stopped my efforts," she explained. "I find I am so drained after only five or ten minutes that I am exhausted. I lost about fifteen pounds in the first few months of doing psychokinetic experiments."

Felicia, who is thirty-seven, discovered her ability in an unusual way. She saw a movie about Nina Kulagina moving objects by mindpower and decided to try it herself. After four months, she was getting nowhere. Then one night she received a telephone call saying that her grandmother was seriously ill. Emotionally upset, she reached for a small bottle in which she kept, of all things, her false eyelashes. It skidded away from her. She snatched it up, shaken. Later, she tried the experiment again. The bottle moved again.

"I obtain these effects only by an emotional buildup," she said. "I concentrate on the object until the most important thing in the world to me is to get it to move. It calls for a tremendous physical effort, too, such an effort that I can hardly speak afterward."

During experimental sessions, Felicia perspires freely. Her eyes and nose run. She shakes with effort as she moves her hands close to the object that she wishes to move. The experiments are obviously an ordeal for her. Curiously, Felicia has the same chronic leg complaint suffered by Nina Kulagina, and again like Nina, Felicia has hyperacute vision.

Felicia has also displayed astonishing powers of clairvoyance. In a series of dream tests, she told of a traffic accident on the Verazzano Bridge, Staten Island; that night, a friend of hers was involved in a motorcycle accident there. Another time, she told of a dream in which she saw her grandmother sitting on the floor in a pool of blood; that night her grandmother fell, cutting her forehead.

For all her abilities, the only testing Felicia has undergone has been voluntary, unpaid, at underfinanced laboratories run by scientists who are never sure how they will meet next year's budget. Let us hope that some government agency is really spending money to find out what is going on in the Soviet Union. Psychic warfare could be more devastating than atomic warfare....

The Psychic Arms Buildup

Armaggedon might well be fought, not with nuclear weapons, but far worse, with mental powers. Many accounts tell of secret studies that are being conducted by Soviet and American governments on the use of psychic weapons and warfare.

In midsummer 1977 I listened to a laser physicist in Santa Monica, California, calmly detail the scientific explanation of frightening psychic powers that he and his team had discovered in a CIA-funded study. The conclusions of that report, which were classified until a few months earlier, were that the Soviets were at least five years ahead of the United States in a race to perfect weapons for psychic warfare. The Soviets had the potential to kill the President of the United States or any other military leader by mindpower alone, and from thousands of miles away, and they were also developing incredible techniques of psychic spying.

At the time, I shook my head in disbelief. But then I read a confidential report obtained in Israel from three Soviet defectors. They claimed that the Soviets were carrying out deadly plans to give them the upper hand in a cold war of the mind.

The defectors are three former researchers in parapsychology. They tell of Tibetan monks trained in the sophisticated use of psychic energy. These men are masters of telekinesis. They can move another person's spinal column and snap it—merely by the power of thought. And distance is no protection. They can kill from a range of thousands of miles. According to the three defectors, other trained psychics are working to monitor thoughts, to communicate with a telephathic "receiver" anywhere in the world, even in places where radio signals cannot reach, such as under the ocean.

In a bizarre application of the mindpowers of psychics, both the CIA research team and the defectors claimed that the Soviets are using psychics to wreck delicate electronic machinery. Such actions would permit them to destroy missile guidance systems, erase computer command tapes, and generally sabotage the U.S. network of defense against nuclear attack.

More personally, one account related by a defector told how he had seen a psychic in a laboratory put a pistol on a table in one room, walk into the next room, and concentrate. "Suddenly," the witness said, "the same pistol materialized in his hand."

Other psychics, some of them KGB officers, are receiving training from the Tibetans, to enable them to crack skulls by thought alone.

And in a more subtle version of psychic warfare, teams of Soviet psychics are working to infuse inanimate objects with feelings of hatred, confusion, and fear. Then these psychically "poisoned" objects—often such simple things as model Sputniks, dolls, or wooden spoons—are given to top Western diplomats as souvenirs. These objects have an effect on the person who handles them. For example, a decision-making diplomat could be made weak and indecisive simply by the "voodoo" or energy-soaked doll on his desk.

Jeff Eerkens, a laser physicist and nuclear engineer who was a member of the five-man team that worked in secret for the CIA on monitoring Soviet psychic research, says: "The principles for psychic warfare are fairly simple, now that we understand something of psychic functioning. The danger is that the Soviets are so far ahead that they could always be able to hide what they are doing from us. It is so dangerous that it is like the atomic bomb. It might sound like science fiction, but it has a real basis in fact."

Dr. Eerkens and his team at Airesearch, in Los Angeles, believe that the Soviets are using machinery to enhance psychic powers. The Airesearch task, for CIA contract XG 4208(54-20)75S, was to study Soviet literature and draw conclusions about what stage the Soviet research is in today. They were also to try, in their year-long study, to produce an explanation for psychic powers.

Says Eerkens: "We got suspicious of the Soviets' work when we found that all the important stuff stopped by 1970. Only rubbish was being published after that. All their top people vanished. So we studied what we had, and we produced a theory for psychic functioning, and we made some projections as to where the Soviets are today. And we were frightened."

Those projections were studied by the CIA, which said that other secret information in its possession showed that their projections were accurate.

The Airesearch team concluded that Russian researchers have a massive secret program under way. It is closely guarded and gets top priority. To add verisimilitude to their statements, the week that I was in California talking to the Airesearch study group, an American newsman was arrested in Russia by the KGB for trying to obtain a copy of a parapsychology scientific paper. The newsman was expelled from the Soviet Union.

Portions of the U.S. team's report concluded that the Soviets already may have mind weapons that could:

- brainwash President Carter from a distance, without anyone's suspecting it.

- kill government or military leaders by thought waves that will induce heart attacks, brain hemorrhages, or madness
- monitor a diplomat's inner feelings against his will
- send messages around the world without wires, satellites, or more power than a small radio uses
- clean vital computer tapes or destroy electronic circuitry
- make objects move by mindpower alone, by destroying the force of friction

Team members also believe that the Soviets have machines that use hynosis to train psychics and other machinery that teaches them to spy on people thousands of miles away, by mindpower alone.

What supporting evidence is there for these fantastic claims?

Item: In April 1976 I spoke to individuals at the Pentagon's Advanced Research Projects Agency in Washington, D.C. They were sponsoring to the tune of $1 million a year, a five-year program, which started in 1973, to monitor brainwaves without attaching electrodes. In other words, they were trying to read the human mind, using a computer.

In 1975, in his annual report and budget to Congress, the director of ARPA, George Heilmeier, admitted that the program was successful. They had been able to identify specific words in a neural language; moreover, "these words have been used with 90% accuracy to interpret what a person is thinking." The United States is working on machines to monitor a person's emotional state.

Item: Rochelle Medici, of the University of California at Los Angeles Brain Research Institute, has been working on animals with electrical fields. Dr. Medici found that "electricity seems to enhance certain brain rhythms.... We might someday be able to help people in learning by tuning into a possible intellectual brain rhythm." Or perhaps, by beaming the wrong frequency, to brainwash a subject?

Item: Psychic Ingo Swann, in a carefully controlled experiment at the Stanford Research Institute, affected a magnetometer encased in copper and steel shielding when it was more than twenty feet away from him and underground. With an electrical or mechanical boost, could not a talented psychic like Swann also effect electronic circuitry?

Item: American as well as Soviet psychics have already documented their ability to move objects at close range by mindpower. Again, with a booster, couldn't they do the same thing at longer ranges?

Item: Avraham Shifrim, former legal adviser to the Soviet Ministry of Defense, now living in Tel Aviv, related the following: Soviet psychics monitor troop movements by mindpower; psychics "poison" objects designed for foreign diplomats' use by sending energies into them; at the Institute of Problems of Translation in Moscow, body chemistry changes are monitored to seek clues to ESP; also at that institute are Tibetan priests who are said to be able to crack skulls, snap spinal columns, and induce heart attacks by mindpower alone.

Item: Dr. Eerkens advised me: "Using extremely low-frequency radiowaves, you could turn on a signal on the same frequency as somebody's brainwaves (once you know what they are) so powerfully that you could make the man go mad. Or you could brainwash him, telling him, 'This is good, this is good.' Or you could send his brain a signal that it didn't know how to cope with, thereby cause the brain to hemorrhage. Perhaps you could even induce heart attacks."

Item: According to Dr. Eerkens, the CIA-sponsored team had worked out the principles needed to send thought waves around the world, using a natural, extremely low-frequency current of electricity that circles the globe at the speed of light. "You could develop a 'psychic radio' that would use this natural force, and you could develop a finely tuned radio-like machine to receive them, too."

Item: In 1975, two Soviet parapsychologists came to Uri Geller's hotel in Milan to conduct tests on him. All the while he was doing his ESP demonstration, they were monitoring him remotely without electrodes, from a suitcase of equipment. "I think they were monitoring my brainwaves," he said. "I was scared." Was this one of the Soviet prototype ESP machines?

Item: Raphael Zidovetski works as a biophysicist at Israel's famous Weitzmann Institute. He was a Soviet parapsychologist. He says: "We were sent out to look for some of the famous Russian witches, because they are probably powerful psychics. With the psychics Nikolaiev and Kamensky, we showed that, by using a system similar to Morse code, they could transfer words, even over long distances. In one experiment, Kamensky imagined he was beating Nikolaiev, who was connected to scientific monitoring devices. The monitors showed how his blood pressure and adrenalin went up, and he got a headache and suffered nausea."

Zidovetski also reports: "In a laboratory in the Zykh Peninsula, near Baku, the Soviets are experimenting in breaking the tip of the spinal column. Distance doesn't matter."

Item: Charles Tart, a professor of psychology at the University of California, Davis, has developed an ESP training machine. Using it, his students beat odds of a million billion billions to one in a statistical study—about the same chance you would have of finding one particular grain of sand on a beach. So it appears as if ESP can be enhanced by machinery or training.

Item: Gottlieb Schneebeli, a Swiss professor of microscopic anatomy at the University of Utah, has found that strong emotions register on a kirlian photography apparatus that he built for $150. This is another example of the ability of machines to monitor human emotions.

Where does all this leave us? Are we lagging far behind in the psychic warfare arena? I asked Dennis Berend, assistant to the director of the Central Intelligence Agency, point-blank: "Do we have a major program underway to investigate psychic functioning?"

Not unreasonably, he refused to answer. "We are running a national intelligence agency here," he said, "not the Wildlife Fund. I couldn't say if we were or if we were not."

Nevertheless, scientists in the field assure me that there is keen CIA interest, and possibly a well-funded program underway. Unlike the Soviets, the CIA is probably funding semi-public research. But the American government agencies, too, are keeping their cards close to their chests. Are some strange happenings the results of their tests—or of psychic warfare?